HEALING THE HEART OF YOUR CHURCH

How Church Leaders Can Break the Pattern of Historic Corporate Dysfunction

By Dr. Kenneth Quick

May 2003

Published by ChurchSmart Resources

We are an evangelical Christian publisher committed to producing excellent products at affordable prices to help church leaders accomplish effective ministry in the areas of Church planting, Church growth, Church renewal and Leadership development.

For a free catalog of our resources call 1-800-253-4276.

Cover design by: Julie Becker

ISBN#: 1-889638-43-9

HEALING THE HEART
OF YOUR CHURCH

To Diane:
my love
my life
my joy
my crown

Table of Contents

Foreword: Healing the Heart of Your Church

by Robert E. Logan

As someone who loves the church and has spent my life working for its well-being and growth, I enthusiastically welcome Kenneth Quick's important contribution to the field of church health and growth. *Healing the Heart of Your Church* addresses a foundational concern: why some churches deal with chronic, seemingly unalterable dysfunction.

As church leaders, we are consistently tempted to look for quick fixes—the latest principle or model that will finally help our church take off and grow. Yet Ken offers us no such band-aids. Because he understands how deep congregational problems can run, he shifts our attention instead to the roots of the problem and encourages us to unearth the deeper issues—the ones we've been afraid to look at. No church growth principle or leadership development strategy will make a lasting difference in our churches if there's undiagnosed disease deep down in the roots.

Unafraid to squarely face the problems of the past, to name the unmentionables—those things that no one talks about but everyone knows—*Healing the Heart of Your Church* offers hope to Christian leaders who count themselves willing to look those painful problems in the eye. Like setting a broken bone, facing the problems of the past will be initially painful, yet brings the possibility of increased health for the future.

It isn't easy dealing with congregational histories that sometimes involve church splits, miscarriages of justice, gross immorality, lack of needed church discipline, or patterns of ignoring serious problems. Ken approaches the task from the perspective of someone who knows how hard it is—someone who's been there and who understands what it's like to live, work, and minister in the messy places where things don't always make sense.

Healing the Heart of Your Church provides empathy for Christian leaders who are worn down by difficulties... yet it doesn't stop there. The book goes on to give practical advice and principles for how to cope with the painful, difficult situations encountered in so many churches. Ken recognizes the various shaping influences on leaders' lives and how that affects their ability or inability to lead in specific situations. He discusses the mediatorial leadership role of pastors and church leaders. Using the letters to the seven churches in Revelation as a pattern, he challenges today's church leaders to consider what type of letter Jesus would write to their congregations—a healthy exercise for any church to work through honestly.

Written not from the ivory tower of theory, but from the down-to-earth, everyday reality of churches, *Healing the Heart of Your Church* makes a valuable contribution to church health and growth by inspiring the courage to go deeper. Once the hidden, underlying problems have been addressed and finally put to rest, congregations are then freed to walk the path of healing and revitalization. If you are ministering in a situation that seems hopeless, if all the leadership and church growth principles you've tried seem to be failing, if your admonitions toward change fall on consistently deaf ears, open yourself up to the message of *Healing the Heart of Your Church*. You may yet find hope.

Introduction

THE STUPIDEST IDEA GOD EVER HAD?

Imagine this: you are part of a denomination that sets forth the following policy: At the end of forty years, every church must disband and sell its property. If the congregation stays together, it must move locations, change names, and develop a new church constitution and a new vision for its ministry. Although I might have trouble signing up churches for such a denomination, I have no doubt that I would have a boatload of frustrated pastors and church lay leaders ready to join.

The statistics documenting pastoral unhappiness and frustration are everywhere. Most surveys indicate that eight out of ten pastors (and eight and a half out of ten pastor's wives) consider themselves discouraged in the ministry, and most lay leaders on church boards find the experience of church leadership detrimental to their spiritual health.

Believe me, I am a full supporter of all the people and ministries whose calling is to help churches grow, but there are times when I have found their messages discouraging in the extreme. They certainly don't intend to discourage me, but the struggle to get my church untracked and moving in the direction these visionaries tell me I should has created times of deep frustration. My response at many pastors conferences I attended and/or books on church growth/vision/pastoral leadership I read was to scream out at the speaker or writer, "I have tried all this and it *did not work*! Not in *my* church!" As I have talked with many of you, my peers, I know I am not alone in my frustration.

Again let me say that vision-casting, church growth and purposeful principles are not wrong or even inappropriate to teach in their context. After twenty-three years in pastoral ministry, I am now a seminary professor and I do teach them. Moreover, I believe we should honor the people in ministry to whom God has given the ten talents when they make ten talents more.

The church DOES need these principles and it needs leaders who know how to live by them and who fulfill their calling to equip the rest of us in what they have learned.

However, there are many of us who have tried our very best to live and implement these things in our ministries. Instead of ever expanding, growing, vibrant churches, we found ourselves bloodied, hurting, discouraged, maybe even changing churches. To the best of our prayerful abilities we tried to apply these principles and they did not work. We ran into inexplicable road-blocks in our church. We end up feeling that we slept through the seminary class or skipped the seminar, the one that provides the key. To contemplate the alternative is worse: we are illustrations of the Peter Principle and have found the level of our incompetence.

The difference between success and us. Many of the super ministry success stories come from church plants where the founding pastors have been a part of the vision and growth from the beginning. However, in many small, medium and large churches, *there were problems rooted in the church's history and pattern of behaving before we ever got there*. This history and these behaviors derail any leadership attempt to lead the church to significant church growth. The frustrated pastor usually has no clue where that brick wall came from or how it got there, and certainly no idea how to remove it.

We enter these churches where bad things have happened with previous pastors, boards, influencers in the congregation over the course of one, two, three decades or more. It becomes like a sick inheritance whose repercussions the new pastor slowly begins to experience. Any number of traumatic things could have happened — splits, moral failures, power plays by board members, spiritual abuse — to wound the corporate heart of this church, and little has been done to heal its wounds or right its wrongs. The premise of this book is that *the Lord of the Church does not let much else happen corporately— dynamic spiritual growth, God's kind of love demonstrated in relationships, revival or renewal, to name a few—until these wrongs are righted and the wounds receive attention*.

This crucial work of assessing and healing the corporate heart of a church, when bypassed, can derail the chance to achieve any other purposes and goals in ministry that church leaders might have. Moreover, if we miss this step in the process, we may have to kiss our health or our joy in ministry goodbye.

I confess this to be my experience. Our church leadership worked several years to develop and carefully craft an elegant, exciting vision for our church. It was so very beautiful! Suffice it to say this elegant vision crashed and burned on the rocks and my ministry lay beside it for several years. I do not have one of those happy "birth-death-fulfillment" stories either. It remained on the rocks and no phoenix rose from the ashes. I watched the godly lay people, who had committed themselves to volunteer long hours on the project, devastated as well. They, like I, were clueless as to why this happened.

We are not alone in our frustration even in our churches. The previous pastor(s), if they did not cause the problem, probably ran into the same road-blocks. *Some reason exists* for why the church is not larger. Something caused the previous pastor to leave. Seldom are these reasons happy ones. Key church leaders are burned, too. You know the statistics. Most people on church boards also find church ministry detrimental to their spiritual lives. Something is wrong with this picture!

The solution of the Siren's song. These good people have had their hearts, spirits and sometimes even their health broken on the rocks of discouragement. They either left the ministry altogether or heard the sweet Siren's song of a new church opportunity that looked better than the frus-trating, painful place they were — the place you may now be ministering!

Pastors in pain regularly read the Siren-like ads like this one, slightly modified from an actual *Christianity Today* ad:

Senior Pastor Desired
Medium-size interdenominational church seeks experienced pastor to lead the church on the path God has set for her. We have warm and teachable people, vibrant lay-led children's and youth programs, an excellent, spiritually-sensitive worship team, a passionate group waiting to be trained in evangelism, and a large, stately, functional, paid-for building in an urban/suburban setting. Six-figure salary for the right man.

The experienced among us know that truth-in-advertising should require this ad to read:

Senior Pastor Barely Tolerated
Medium-size (read "75") Bapto-Metho-Presbo-First-Assembly-South-of-God-Bible church seeks experienced (read "breathing") pastor to lead the church on the path God has set for her (Ha Ha—too many jokes here). We have warm (read "neither hot nor cold") and teachable (add "when they are awake") people, vibrant (read "burned-out") lay-led (read "expect to have to take this over")

children's and youth programs, an excellent, spiritually-sensitive worship team (read "you better do it their way or else"), a passionate group waiting to be trained in evangelism (HaHaHaHa, heehee), and a large (read "ugly"), stately (read "old"), functional (read "empty"), paid-for (read "really really old") building in an urban/suburban (read "reclamation area") setting. Six-figure salary for the right man (read $8,257.34).

I had one pastor in pain tell me that, when things are bad, he reads the want ads with longing and the obituaries with envy. I had another pastor look me in the eye and say with all the force that his frustration could muster, "The church was the *stupidest idea* God ever had!" Broken hearts, broken spirits, broken dreams of seeing God's church grow and advance are behind such statements.

The objective of this book. So what can I contribute to help alleviate this pain? I want to encourage these normally positive people who have given up so much to do what they do. I will propose a process that holds hope for them as leaders, something that will strengthen them spiritually and possibly even set their church free to become all God intended it to be!

Let me state my belief plainly: Within many churches, especially those that have been in existence for a while, there are some *God-designed preconditions* that must be met before vision casting and church growth principles can become effective. This is universally true for churches that have *painful* histories. I also believe few churches escape painful crises just as few people do. Moreover, I believe God speaks to a corporate church body during such painful times and seeks to teach them *corporate lessons*. A pastor must help the church lay leaders determine what these corporate lessons have been. I believe local churches are usually stuck until they discern these divine instructions and make changes according to the will of God.

Learning how to do this is the essence of this book. *You must assess and address some historical spiritual roadblocks that are in the way before you can lead your church to healthy church growth*. It takes a good, solid, thoughtful kind of spiritual leadership to do these things. I believe God uniquely equips those in spiritual authority — pastors and lay leaders with them — to give this kind of leadership, to be proactive not reactive. A pastor can not address these historical issues without growing and developing both insight and understanding of the way the church works and the way God works in the church.

Guarantees I can not make. I wish I could guarantee the process would be painless or easy. It sure wasn't for me. It grieves me to think of adding one iota of pain to some of you. However, I can say unequivocally that this will be *a good kind of pain*, the pain of setting a bone, of removing an abscess — the kind of pain you endure to get stronger, not the kind pastors are often enduring. I am not talking about the pain of a growing ulcer, a deteriorating spine or a ministry going nowhere for inexplicable reasons.

I can not guarantee your church will change at the end of the process, that you will have a positive testimony of change like God in His mercy has given me. Ultimately, like the Israelites at Kadesh-Barnea, your people will make their choice whether to follow God against the obstacles from their history. They may want to go back to their equivalent of Egypt and slavery. God's desire will be clear. No one blames Moses' lack of leadership for the Israelites choice to be cowardly at that crucial moment. Congregations make choices that pastors and church leaders cannot control. God allows it. I hope that when the time comes and God makes clear what to do, your congregation senses God's clear call to act and everyone will have the courage to obey. You and your leaders are responsible to bring them to the border of that possibility.

Nor can I promise the process will be rapid, though it may surprise you how quickly things turn around. However, I can guarantee that 1) if you learn to discern what God has been trying to teach you and your church by some of the painful things it (and you) have been through, and 2) if you do what God wants you to do about it, then 3) you will personally experience divine confirmation and freedom. Your church will experience a release of God's Spirit as the healing takes place in its heart. No one obeys what God has been trying to teach him/her without God's visible blessing and reinforcement. That's when all the vision-casting seminars and church growth books may begin to help you.

One more item—this is not a book on church discipline. In the course of your work through this book, you may come across individuals from your church's past who should have been disciplined. They may still be in your church! The purpose of this book isn't to counsel you on what to do in the variety of situations you are apt to find. Instead this book will guide you on how to go about addressing the corporate issues that remain after a failure to discipline.

Well, there it is. I know you may be cynical and weary of people giving you advice. I do not blame you. You can hold all this at arm's length as you evaluate it. That's okay. I sure would. I just appreciate the heart that loves God enough not to quit yet. I admire the person who still feels that mysterious call deep in the soul to hang in there, still feels motivated enough to try to solve ministry's puzzles. Enough to pick up yet another book that holds the potential to frustrate.

It is my prayer that this time the results will be quite different.

— CHURCH CARDIOLOGY —

Chapter 1

THE CONCEPT OF THE CORPORATE HEART

Once while watching Monday Night Football, I heard Al Michaels describe a condition clearly evident on the field. The home team (I forget who), behind by ten points with four minutes left in the game, had just driven the length of the football field and were at the one yard line. The fans were going nuts! Two runs failed to get in the end zone and on third down, the quarterback dropped back and threw a bullet of a pass. The ball hit the receiver in the chest and bounced into the air. A defensive back snatched it and ran it back 102 yards for a touchdown. Michaels described the situation: "When he intercepted and ran back that pass, it took the heart right out of the team. It broke their back." We know what he referred to. You could see the sagging shoulders of the players, the corporate sadness of the home team. It was not just individuals at the moment who were sad, it was the team. Indeed the whole stadium joined them in misery (except on the opposing sideline).

The idea that a team, a group, a community, and even a country could have a single heart or spirit impacted by events is not a new revelation. Does that somehow relate to what we often see in churches? We would probably not have a problem believing that the report of a beloved woman in the church receiving a diagnosis of inoperable cancer would cause a "corporate heart" response of concern and sadness in the church. Is the same "corporate heart" responding when it appears that everyone has suddenly become suspicious of a board proposal? We must address the question: Is the idea of a "corporate heart" in the church biblical? The answer to that question begins with understanding the church as a Body.

A "system of systems." When we think about a human body, we realize it is *a system of systems*, a set of interdependent systems–muscular, skeletal, circulatory, nervous, etc.–wondrously woven into a working whole. Sickness or danger to one part affects the whole. Each part should work properly and proper working means its interdependence and linkage to other parts. If the hand does not pull the nail out of the foot, if the mouth does not call for help when drowning, if the eyes, brain, muscles and feet do not work together to stop for the red light, every body part is in trouble!

The New Testament teaches us to think, not just of the universal Church, but of the local church as an organic whole, a "body." The Church in recent decades has rejoiced to rediscover "body-life," the importance of believers operating with their spiritual gifts and contributing their unique ministries to the Church. However, we should apply the same principles to corporate sin, sickness and wounds. We see how Jesus does this in His letters to the seven churches of Revelation.

Revelation 2 and 3. It took me a while to grasp the biblical concept of corporateness, steeped as I was in individualistic thinking, but when I did, a lot of other things crystallized as well. I base the concept of a corporate heart for a local church on the seven letters Jesus sent to the seven churches in Revelation 2 and 3. In these letters He evaluates their *corporate histories*. "I know your [sing.] works" is His common refrain. These "works" are behaviors and attitudes He sometimes commends ("your [sing.] love, faith, service, and patient endurance. I know that your [sing.] last works are greater than the first." Rev. 2:19). He states these clearly individual behaviors as singular corporate actions. He also sometimes rebukes them corporately ("Wake up, and strengthen what remains and is on the point of death, for I have not found your [sing.] works perfect in the sight of my God. Remember then what you [sing.] received and heard; obey it, and repent" 3:2,3).

I do not know about you, but I find this concept rather startling. In Jesus' view of a *local* church, individual members recede and He sees a single body. Jesus sees the collective actions and attitudes of church members as a *singular whole*. He defines each local church as a single entity with commendable works or failings that require a singular corporate repentance and obedience. We do not have to guess the role church leaders of these seven churches would play in this. *They would be responsible to confront the problems He addresses and lead the changes.* End of story.

Jesus knows our church. Jesus knows who and what we have in our churches. He would be aware of the new believers who are still struggling to break sinful habits from their unconverted days, the spiritual toddlers trying to learn how to walk by taking tumbles over temptation daily. He would see the things those who look godly on the outside have going on in secret. That was all happening back in Ephesus and Sardis too. All of it. Those churches would all have had their core groups, their less committed groups, their peripheral groups. They would have had people coming and going. He *still* speaks of these local churches as if a single entity, a body by itself.

Occasionally Jesus does mention individuals in these seven letters ("Yet you have still a few persons in Sardis who have not soiled their clothes; they will walk with me, dressed in white, for they are worthy"). Their association with the church does not condemn those individuals who are not caught up in whatever evil occurs within the church. Personal responsibility still matters. I am not lessening it at all. Yet even when individuals appear in this context, the corporate impact still concerns Jesus most. He still recommends corporate action. Thus the Lord teaches those of us in church leadership this corporate way to view our church.

Corporate response to corporate problems. The apostle Paul addressed nine of his thirteen letters to churches with corporate problems. Only occasionally does he mention specific problem people. Most problems are presented as a *corporate concern*. The one immoral man in Corinth caused the apostle to rebuke the whole congregation for its lack of appropriate corporate response. "And you are arrogant! Should you not rather have mourned, so that he who has done this would have been removed from among you?" (1 Cor. 5:2)

When was the last time your whole congregation mourned the sinfulness of one of its members? It's hard to picture this in some of our megachurches. I would guess that the democratic philosophies of the Greeks would have impacted the Corinthians the same way we in North America have felt them. "Not *my* problem!" they thought. The apostle calls this arrogance, to believe somehow we are not a part of the problem. The sin of the one has injured the *body*. The local church of Corinth stepped on the spiritual equivalent of a rusty nail, hurtful to a small area but potentially destructive to the whole. This wound calls for a corporate emotional response – mourning – and corporate action. Everyone should feel it.

Why? What will happen if the corporate body does not respond? Paul tells them: "Do you not know that a little yeast leavens the whole batch of dough? Clean out the old yeast so that you may be a new batch, as you really are unleavened. For our paschal lamb, Christ, has been sacrificed" (1 Cor. 5:6-7). Christ has provided the means by His sacrifice of cleaning out the leaven of our lives, and-hear the apostle-of our churches too. However, this requires corporate action.

Non-corporate response to corporate problems. Sometimes sin becomes embodied in a person and that person becomes a potential danger to the corporate body. What kind of danger? Is the danger in 1 Corinthians 5 that every member of that church will start having sexual relations with their mothers? I do not think so. However, something occurs to damage the corporate spiritual fabric of the congregation that Jesus sees and feels. I believe those in spiritual leadership must also feel this pain in order to be motivated to act upon it. Otherwise the leaders experience that "frog-in-the-kettle" desensitizing to something spiritually lethal.

Now everyone in our congregation grapples with sin daily and feels bad about it most of the time. As a pastor, I am grappling too. I do not think the apostle refers to this normal daily struggle, but to the public, deliberate acts of someone or some group who flaunts God's grace without any regret. More importantly I believe he refers to corporate attitudes and actions that stain the church indelibly.

Let's move to your church in the twenty-first century. What if this travesty was committed twenty years ago and your church's leadership never dealt with it? What if thirty years ago the pastor was immoral, almost everyone knew about the immorality, but he was quietly asked to leave with nothing more said? If fifteen years ago a deacon absconded with your church's funds? If twenty-five years ago there was a nasty church split? If fifty years ago your church looked away and never commented as a mob lynched a black teenager one night on the lot across the street? Do these things affect the corporate spiritual fabric of your church? Does time cause the stains to fade? Would it surprise you if it did not; if the spiritual poison kneaded into the corporate body at that time still spins out painful repercussions? No one ever led the church to deal with the issue. Whoever should have taken responsibility for these things before God, to confess them corporately and take steps to rectify the damage, never did so.

The church as a "body." The Bible describes the local and universal Church as a body, but the idea of the singular "heart" of a local church might be a new concept. In Revelation 2 and 3, however, Jesus uses a singular pronoun "you" both to commend and admonish each church. Jesus expects that the church will hear and respond from its singular corporate heart. He says to the Ephesian church,

"Yet I hold this against you (sing.): You (sing.) have forsaken your (sing.) first love. Remember the height from which you (sing.) have fallen! Repent and do the things you (sing.) did at first. If you (sing.) do not repent, I will come to you (sing.) and remove your lampstand from its place." (Rev. 2:4,5 NIV)

Let's admit it; most of us in the West have trouble with this kind of thinking. Certainly we struggle with how to operate this way. In North America particularly we are immersed in the philosophies and values of individualism. "If it isn't my problem, then it isn't my problem." That thinking simply doesn't work in a body. Listen to Paul in Ephesians 4:11-13:

It was he who gave some to be apostles, some to be prophets, some to be evangelists, and some to be pastors and teachers, to prepare God's people for works of service, so that the body of Christ may be built up until we all reach unity in the faith and in the knowledge of the Son of God and become mature, attaining to the whole measure of the fullness of Christ. (NIV)

Here he describes the work of spiritual leadership in helping individual saints contribute to the growth of the corporate body. The ultimate goal of the individual effort is the corporate singular good—the shared unity of faith and knowledge, the maturity of the singular entity, the final measure being a church that operates with the fullness of Jesus in it and through it.

When the "body" gets sick. Though there are many things that can derail such a lofty goal, Paul explains what can keep them on corporate track in Ephesians 4:15,16:

Instead, speaking the truth in love, we will in all things grow up into him who is the Head, that is, Christ. From him the whole body, joined and held together by every supporting ligament, grows and builds itself up in love, as each part does its work. (NIV)

We are to become corporately all Christ intends by the proper working of each individual part *at the local church level.* So now a "body part," a deacon for instance, has an affair with another body part, say the choir director. Though people come to know this, no one addresses it publicly. The leadership quietly asks the two to leave and many think nothing more needs to happen. A key joint and ligament in the body have just been discovered to be cancerous. The knee-jerk response is to remove the parts without proper treatment.

Many churches operate by the principle "out of sight, out of mind." It's not our problem any more. Only that joint and ligament were a part of the local body. Can a church ignore such a problem without corporate effects? The only additional questions I would ask are: What if it happened fifteen years ago? Is it possible that over the last fifteen years the corporate body would have continued to feel the effects of it? Might Jesus have it on His list of things the corporate body had tolerated inappropriately? A country gospel song called "One More Time around Mt. Sinai" captures the danger. The thrust of this comic-tragic song is that, like Israel's wilderness wanderings, God keeps taking His people around and around through similar experiences until they finally learn the lessons that allow them to make further progress. Could that explain your church's problems in the present? Are they taking yet again another trip around Mt. Sinai?

What you do not know can kill you. Such a shift in thinking has astounding implications to church leaders. What the pastor does not know about the corporate entity, what the church lay leaders and the pastor do not corporately address, can kill their vision for ministry, their church, their pastor or all the above.

How does this happen? I picture a pastor called to the church at Thyatira attempting to get this church off the mark down the purpose-driven highway. All the while an undealt-with influencer poisons the heart of the Thyatiran church. Or perhaps God calls him to the church at Ephesus. He does not sense, in light of the strong doctrinal statement and wide-ranging ministries this church has, that something happened in its history—a "fall" Jesus says—that will shortly remove that church's lamp from its lampstand unless recti-fied. These pastors and their church leadership must rightly assess this, address it *corporately* and repent before the full purposes of Christ can be realized.

How do pastors and church leaders begin to do this?

Summary. Jesus spoke to the seven local churches of Revelation 2 and 3 about present spiritual problems rooted in their historical choices. He used the singular pronoun "you" to address those congregations, indicting or praising each local church as a single entity. This is the basis for under-standing the concept of the corporate heart. Your local church is a singular entity before Christ. He not only addresses individuals and works in them, He addresses the corporate body about what is happening in its heart as well. Entering a church without understanding its history and what Jesus is speaking to corporately can cause a pastor a lot of pain.

Chapter 2

GROUNDWORK: THE HEART OF THE LEADER OF CHURCH LEADERS

Socrates gets credit for saying, "The unexamined life is not worth living." Maybe a tad overstated, but probably not much. I believe failing to examine one's life does make living harder and leaves a lot in a life inexplicable. I came to this discovery through a very different kind of examination. Here is what I concluded.

A pastor's four interdependent relationships. There are four "family" relationships that govern a pastor's, or any church leader's, experience in church ministry, four "forces"—as family is a force in our lives—that pull or push him emotionally and spiritually. For the process to be totally effective, a pastor needs to do a thorough evaluation of what is going on in these four family relationships. They are all interconnected, though we generally do not feel the interconnection. The following visual illustrates these interconnections.

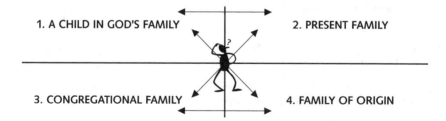

I do not intend this book to provide a complete analysis of the dynamics of all four of these quadrants, any one of which could be the subject of a book. The reality is, however, that *they are all constantly at work* influencing responses and reactions to each other. However, some go deeper than others.

Problems here = problems there. For instance, the present frustration of a pastor (or a lay leader for that matter) to solve conflict in his congregation (quadrant 3) may cause the revisiting of an "ancient frustration" from his family of origin (quadrant 4). By way of example, growing up as the eldest child in an alcoholic home, the child-now-pastor felt responsible to keep things "normal" for his siblings while mom or dad or both were drunk. He was not always successful because he felt his siblings would not cooperate with him. As a child he felt both crushing responsibility and total helplessness in the face of this chaos. Now he feels the *exact same* frustration and powerlessness in the church family as it grapples with its problems. Seldom, if ever, does he connect his childhood experience of pain with his pastoral experience. He does not realize he has always felt responsible for bringing order, direction and health to a chaotic "family." This new "family" typically does not cooperate either, leaving him feeling impotent, like a failure.

What compounds this pain is that he senses that God (quadrant 1) likewise holds him responsible, and that he is therefore failing God by his inability to improve his church situation. He relives the *exact same* pain in his relationship with God. Add into this, a belief—common for children of alcoholics—that he cannot count on God when it matters most, just like his alcoholic parent. Many pastors struggle with a relational image of God far different than their theological and doctrinal image. The god they relate to, shaped less by the Scriptures than their life experience, is unreliable or worse.

Thus the pastor experiencing bad times in the church (quadrant 3) uses his life experiences in his birth family to translate them emotionally (quadrant 4). When he cannot right things, he believes he fails God (quadrant 1). Do you think his wife and children (quadrant 2) escape his inability to cope with these things in the other three quadrants? They are all interconnected. His history colors the present experiences and responses.

This scenario is one of a zillion. The child-now-pastor could have grown up without affection, experienced abandonment, or had hyper-controlling parents. He could have been sexually abused or never able to make his dad happy. All have their parallels in the experience within the church family.

God's work to heal. Here is where we see how marvelous God is. I believe God sovereignly works on the church to heal its corporate heart. He has ordered circumstances to communicate where there are problems. However, God in His love and mercy is *also at work in the pastor's heart* ordering circumstances to help heal his own heart from ancient wounds. As the pastor revisits his own ancient pain, he experiences a call, an invitation, a summons from his heavenly Father who loves him and knows every single thing about his past and present.

Elijah heard it as a question while he sat depressed in Sinai's cave. God asked simply "What are you doing here, Elijah?" Didn't God know? Of course He knew. God was summoning Elijah to reflect on how he ended up this way. I believe God invited him to leave an ancient "way of pain." At his worst suicidal moment Elijah confesses "I am no better than my fathers" (1 Kings 19:4), a reference probably to the cowardly actions of Israel at Kadesh mirrored in his fleeing before Jezebel. Such a thought has frozen many a man of God in his tracks, realizing that he now repeats the sins of his relatives in his present life and ministry. God asks him the question to summon him out of that way of pain.

Discovering the pathways of pain. David prays for such knowledge in Psalm 139. This Psalm reinforces the infinite intimacy of God's knowledge of his life and thoughts, of exactly where he is on any map you care to name. David ends his song with a cry for revelation:

Search me, O God, and know my heart;

Test me and know my anxious thoughts.

See if there is any offensive way (lit. 'way, path of pain') in me,

And lead me in the way everlasting. (Ps. 139:23,24 NIV)

This "pathway of pain" has been the subject of renewed interest because of the Prayer of Jabez in 1 Chronicles 4:10. Jabez prays using the same Hebrew word as David "that I may not cause pain." David's cry here is not that *God* would know his ways of pain, but that God would reveal them to *David*!

These "pathways of pain" are sometimes the sinful repeated habits of our hearts and minds. We have beaten down these pathways by repeated activities and attitudes that we know cause us pain and from which we must repent. I believe David knows that the pathways of pain also included ways of reacting and responding to circumstances that are not godly either. These other painful paths may have been beaten down long ago in the context of our families. God may graciously heal some hearts completely at the time of salvation, but for others, these painful patterns are left like thorns in the flesh, messengers from Satan to buffet us.

I personally believe that God constantly summons His children away from these "paths of pain" toward "eternal paths," His paths, the paths of peace. Emotional paths of pain are far less recognizable in our lives than sinful paths. They are so much a part of the fabric of our lives and thinking, it is hard to view them objectively. We have lived with them so long, we cannot conceive of life without them. Like the trenches one can still see as remnants of World War I in France, our ancient defenses remain scarring the landscape of our lives long after the painful battles of childhood are over.

Therefore, they need God's searching and revealing work to show us exactly what is going on. How would God do this so we might recognize it? Pain. The kind of pain that looks at obituaries with envy. Exactly that kind.

Let me share one of my paths of pain derived from quadrant 4 that resulted in major problems as a pastor. Though I believe my parents loved each other deeply (a great heritage), they were not perfect. They brought baggage into their marriage and parenting from their own childhood experience. My father's family had a history of alcoholism. The men tended to be weak and the women strong, often holding the families together. Limited emotional resources meant that he grew up learning that he must avoid conflict at all costs. Conflicts drained the family of the energy necessary to cope and survive.

My mother grew up on a farm in the Depression and somehow got the message she needed to be responsible for her whole family's needs, which were many. She was strong but she carried enormous guilt if she failed to carry out these responsibilities to her high internal standard. This constant inner pressure, I believe, resulted in a fiery temper at times, frightening to me as a child. I would do almost anything to keep her from getting angry.

I watched my parents dance their dance, two people who clearly loved each other, but both struggling with the impact of their own upbringing. My father struggled to carry responsibility, particularly financial responsibility, to the level my mother needed to feel safe. He also had trouble (as do many children of alcoholics) asking for what he needed. My mother felt the pressure of responsibility having to carry the family. There were seldom conflicts between my parents, because there was no "between." My mother might become angry at something and my father, rather than fight, would usually absorb her anger and withdraw to end it. Therefore fights (which require at least two) were few and far between.

I learned two things here that became paths of pain for me. One was to fear anger—my own or anyone else's, but particularly feminine anger. The second was to absorb anger or placate the angry one, in whatever way I could, in order to stop it. Here was my "ancient" defense system constructed when I was a child. It continued when I got married (quadrant 2). I feared my wife's anger and sought to avoid it at all costs. She became unsafe to me when she was angry. If I could not avoid her anger, I would absorb it.

Rather than assess my responsibility in the situation I regularly just took blame and absorbed the conflict or withdrew to end it. "It's all my fault. I'm sorry," I would whine, often not feeling sorry at all. I just wanted her anger to stop. Of course, martyrs are righteous people, so playing the martyr like this could allow me to feel good while communicating she was wrong for being angry at one so righteous. It isn't hard to understand how this often enflamed her anger, especially if her anger were righteous. She sensed that I was not truly taking any responsibility. However, on my emotional landscape, anger was never righteous, only a fearful thing from which I had to protect myself.

How did this affect my relationship with the church family (quadrant 3)? You can probably guess. I had learned a role, a path of pain, in my birth family that I brought into my marriage and it caused me pain there. Receiving Christ and even entering ministry did not dismantle these ancient coping mechanisms. Walking into a church as its pastor did not make me trust in God one iota more in the area of conflict. In fact, I would say I was totally blind to the destructive role I began to play in the church.

As I began to experience conflict in the church family, I reverted to the single defense mechanism I knew: absorb it like a sponge to end it. Like my father, I also could not ask for what I needed. Early in my ministry or when things were going well, this sponge technique could soak up the little spurts and puddles of conflict quite well. The time came though when church conflict overflowed the banks for a long period. I kept absorbing it, only it began to both depress and burn me out. There was simply too much. I came home one day several years ago and cried to my wife, "I *have* to do something different with my life. I cannot take it anymore!" Instead of approaching the church leadership with what I needed, I wanted to bail out instead.

Now behold God's mercy! My church had learned some major paths of pain, very unhealthy coping mechanisms, related to its history (which I will share later) and so did I. God was revealing *both* of them and summoning us both to the "eternal way" in relation to them. He was speaking both to me, *and* to the corporate body the way He spoke to the churches in Revelation.

The commonness of the pattern. I have become convinced that this path I followed is "common to humans." The pattern is this: God sovereignly arranges for the call of a man with such a problem to a local church with a *similar* struggle. All the while the pastor believes the reason God called him to the church is the mission, the vision and the strategy God wants to fulfill. God meanwhile works to *heal both the church and the pastor* of their paths of pain so that they can fulfill the vision and accomplish the mission. I believe God called me to my church at that time to heal me. By His grace He also healed them.

These healings were not instantaneous. I had groundwork to do, a journey to take, before I could lead my church to heal its heart. I had to discover how to work with God to heal my own heart. Truthfully I was scared to death what such a journey would mean. I had not gone along denying these things in my life because they were painless or simple to handle. The very reason I constructed the defenses and operated the way I did was *I saw no other options*. I did not want to admit to myself or to anyone else that kind of spiritual and emotional weakness. Pastors are supposed to have it all together. I had to admit that I loved the ministry for that reason—I could at least look like I had it together. I *counseled* broken people. I did not want to admit that I belonged in their ranks.

However, healing like this is exactly what God calls us to do—pastors and everyone else—throughout our lives. I was about to learn the power of what Henri Nouwen calls "the wounded healer." No one grows up in a perfect family. No one, nada, zilch, zero. Good—yes, when balanced against evil—many families were good. Positive—yes, many families provided positive experiences for their children; but perfect—no. Otherwise Christ had no reason to die for me for there was nothing for His grace to restore. He heals what the world has broken in the hearts of His sons and daughters, so they can display the wonders of His saving grace and restorative mercy. Pastors are not just instruments of grace and healing to His people in this regard. They are models of how to receive grace and healing as well.

Okay. Where does one start?

Start with your family of origin. For me, logically, the journey started with a map—a map of my family of origin. I needed to understand my roots to understand myself. The generations of my family passed to me weaknesses and strengths as an inheritance. Ultimately this was the same kind of work I would do for the church so it was great preparation. I developed this family map in several key ways.

First, I drew a genealogical family tree (called a "genogram") for several generations back on both sides of my family. Many people do the normal genealogical work and much of this information is probably available in your family. If not, you can become your "family historian." There are a number of books available to help you draw a genogram of your family.[1] I have given some examples of genograms of Abraham's family in the Appendix.

Second, I was not just looking for the things normally found on a genealogical tree. I wanted to map and understand the nature of the relationships between husbands and wives, parents and children, and siblings with each other. I wanted to see if there were addictive behaviors, knowing the power they have to create dysfunction in a family. I looked for tragedies for similar reasons. How families cope with tragedies declares much about their health. I sought to see the patterns of behavior in some crucial relational areas, like conflict and intimacy, all of which would be a clue to my own patterns of behavior. Gender behavior was particularly important. What roles did the women take, what roles did the men take? Were the men good husbands? Good fathers? Did they show favoritism?

Third, I interviewed family members and let them tell me stories about historical events in the family as far back as they could remember. Like Alex Haley in *Roots* I listened for even the vestiges of ancient family stories from maternal and paternal sides, knowing that such stories captured the essence of our family. All families maintain the key "symbolic stories" of the family in their storytelling, stories that symbolize much larger truths about the family. Family members often repeat these stories at holiday gatherings or funerals. My family's stories told me who we were and where we came from, the key people, events and tragedies that had shaped us.

I was not deliberately digging for dirt. Far from it. I sought the true picture, good and bad, nothing denied or soft-soaped. I sought family strengths and victories as well as weaknesses and failings. Nor was I seeking to blame. Blame is a pointless exercise, accomplishing absolutely nothing, a foul inheritance left over from our original parents in the Garden of Eden. It was the first thing Adam and Eve both did when God confronted them with their sinful behavior (Gen. 3:12,13). That, in and of itself, should discourage us from such a path.

In the course of this exercise I sat down with my mother (my father died in 1969) and looked over old photo albums and listened to stories. I spent time with aunts and uncles and recorded their memories and stories about their grandparents and other relatives. I went on a retreat with my two sisters where we combined our knowledge and perspectives of our family and put it into a chronology. I cannot overemphasize the value of this to my life, how it clarified for me who I was and the multigenerational forces that had shaped me and my relationships with my own wife and son.

Examine your marriage next. My own marriage was next on the list. All the historical forces I learned about had shaped me—the good, bad and ugly—as they had shaped my parents and my grandparents. I needed to realize they also continued to shape my marriage, my parenting and my ministry. I saw in my family history reflections of my own behaviors and atti-tudes toward conflict and intimacy, world-view and self-worth, responsibility, explanations for pain and choices about how to cope with pain. I forged all these in the crucible of my family. I needed to allow God to tell me the truth about these things, for many of them had become ways of pain for me. With the Holy Spirit, I had the resources I needed to make the changes necessary. He could help me face my fears and change what I believed could never change.

This task may seem overwhelming, but it isn't. As your own heart finds healing from the ways of pain, you become equipped to lead your church to do the same. They need you to lead them. Your spouse and children need you to lead them, as they are probably caught up in your paths of pain also.

I began to work on my marriage, and the impact of even the smallest of changes stunned me. My wife and I had a good marriage (in both of our evaluations) but my fear of her anger had always been a major problem. I began to choose a different way of relating to her when she was angry. I chose to commit myself into the hands of Christ and not to withdraw emotionally from her or absorb blame. I honestly thought I would die the first several times I stood there and did not play the martyr while her anger washed over me. (Only those of you who learned to fear anger know what I am talking about.) I trusted Christ to keep me, I stayed close to her emotionally, and listened for the things she expressed in her anger for which I felt genuinely responsible. Lo and behold, I did not die! At that moment my wife became much safer to me, and I therefore could be much more intimate with her (the byproduct of safety). Indeed I had never experienced that level of intimacy before. My good marriage became great!

Reflect on your role in the church. A set of specific roles and expectations governs most pastoral ministry within any given church. Like a couple coming to marriage, both the pastor and the "corporate body" have these roles and expectations in the background of their understanding. A pastor and search committee may discuss a few beforehand, but most are discovered afterwards, sometimes quite painfully. Of course, each individual in the church has his/her own set, but seldom do they vary greatly from the corporate norm. Many *forces* go into defining those roles from the church's perspective, and many *experiences* go into defining them for the pastor himself.

The forces shaping these roles differ from congregation to congregation based on a number of factors. *Locale* has much to do with this. The expectations of people in a rural community differ greatly from those in an urban setting. Many pastors run up against this if they move to a church in a different locale, and have to adjust. *Ethnicity* also has an impact. The role expectations in an African-American pastorate will differ from a Korean which will differ from a Caucasian. Another shaping influence is *denominational tradition*, both the denomination of the specific local church or the denominational tradition of a majority of the congregation.

However, of all the factors that determine pastoral roles, *local church history* is the most significant. Why? Because things have happened with previous pastors that have shaped your church's view of pastors and the pastoral role. I remember candidating in my first church and preaching my "best" sermon, as candidates tend to do. My wife, my most trusted critic, confirmed it was the best she had heard. What was interesting is that clearly no one in the church or at the board interview that followed was impressed. Pastors sense such things.

How could they not be impressed? Their history with the previous pastor is the reason. A dynamic preacher, he had very poor interpersonal skills. His final Sunday in the church he called the church a "disgrace to the community." The board met and came to him that afternoon and asked him not to return. The pain of that corporate experience colored their view of my preaching. Unlike most churches, they simply did not trust preaching alone as an indicator of positive ministry. That attitude had a significant impact on my role in the church.

Sometimes people perceive the model of the previous pastor as positive in the sense that they want the next pastor (you) to do the same things. These expectations also can cause a great deal of pressure or pain. I candidated at a church in which I had gotten fairly far through the process. I flew in to interview with the search committee. I had filled out their questionnaires until my head hurt. These people knew more about me than God. I began the interview and early on they told me they noticed my wife was getting her MBA. They thought this was an inappropriate degree for a woman, and since the last pastor's wife ministered beside him and made the church her life, they wanted my wife to do the same. My wife and I worked this through early in ministry—she needed the freedom to operate where God called her and according to her gifts, not in some role the church has carved for her. I fully supported her in this. I told this church "No way!" and, thankfully, they showed me the door. However, I hate to think of the pain that such expectations—all based on history—have caused many pastors who did not hear about them before arriving to take a ministry.

Pastors experience serious emotional trouble when the role expectations of the church clash with the roles the pastor is accustomed to taking in his family. For instance, growing out of my family history as I mentioned earlier, I personally felt that one of my unspoken pastoral roles was to be a shock absorber and conflict sponge. Stop the anger, whatever it costs. Because of my church's history, they unwittingly supported this unspoken role. It was not on my job description, but it was very real and it was killing me. One can only soak up so many bad feelings before one's stomach acid kicks into overdrive.

I also ran into the clash of roles in my first ministry. Again, local church history determined the pattern. The founding pastor was known for always being present at any small or large crisis of any church member, any time day or night. He loved to sit on the porches of people's homes and sip tea and "chat" for hours. His sermons were not as "meaty" as mine, but few cared about that because they knew he loved them. His pattern did not define my ministry priorities. I spent time preparing solid sermons, but subsequently I did not have the same amount of time to do the visitation he did. There was a fair amount of grumbling and unfavorable comparisons between me and the first pastor because I didn't do visitation the way he did. Some people told me this to my face and it was pretty painful.

Reflect on your ministry. How have the previous administrations had an impact on how your church views you? Some of what took place created climates difficult for the next pastors to handle. If you fail to understand completely your role expectations—the ones you carry and the ones the church has—at the beginning of this process of healing the heart of your church, you could miss some major areas for healing.

Summary. There is groundwork that church leaders need to do in their own hearts before they can properly see how to work on the church. Discerning the ways of pain in your church's heart, you need first to understand your own. You need to examine your relational roles in each of the four quadrants. Start with your birth family. Draw a map of the relationships for several generations and identify the problem areas, the "ways of pain" relationally. Then examine your marriage and family to see if you have carried on any of these ways of pain. Courageously address these issues. Finally consider carefully the roles you have taken in your church and the roles they expected you to play. Chances are there are ways of pain here too that have left you either in conflict, depressed or discouraged. All this is preparation for the good work of leadership upon which you are about to embark. God called you to your church to do it. He also had you pick up this book to call you to it.

Such are the ways of God. He has timed it all.

Chapter 3

A GOOD KIND OF SPIRITUAL LEADERSHIP

There are some aspects of church ministry and leadership all pastors would rather not have to face—firing lazy or incompetent staff, dealing with stubborn Board members, receiving a fifteen-page epistle from a church member correcting the pastor's view on baptism, cleaning up after the youth ministry's "mile-long sundae" party, etc. Most pastors sigh and accept these burdens as part of the calling, but look to do things more spiritually profitable. The process I am about to describe is what I call a "good kind of leadership" because it holds the hope of making a profound long-term difference in the direction and growth of your church's ministry. It helps the pastor and church leaders embrace a powerful tool for accomplishing good in the context of ministry, a tool called *mediatorial authority*.

Flock-focused Shepherding. How authority works when exercised over a flock of God's children, particularly spiritual authority, is one of the least understood dynamics in the modern church. This lack of understanding has led to a growing trust in the world's definitions and patterns of leadership. Church leaders have looked to business and the military for their principles of leadership. They read Drucker, Bennis, and Sun Tsu for insights on how to lead and manage their church, staff and people. These teachers do provoke our thinking and have their place, but they are in the category of modern psychology. Psychology is helpful when it observes and describes accurately the way humans relate, but unhealthy and dangerous when it theorizes why humans relate that way. Spiritual leadership is qualitatively different than any business or military model of leadership.

Many abuses to authority also reflect those seen in the world, abuses that Peter describes in 1 Peter 5:2-3.

Be shepherds of God's flock that is under your care, serving as overseers— not because you must, but because you are willing, as God wants you to be; not greedy for money, but eager to serve; not lording it over those entrusted to you, but being examples to the flock. (NIV)

Peter lists three temptations unique to people "in charge:" motivation, money and power. God has a way He wants those in spiritual authority to lead His flock. First, they must want to do it willingly, not because someone, even God, forces them. Second, they must not look to profit on the backs of those they care for, but give themselves to serve from the heart. Third, they must not enjoy the power and control they have over lives, but must model the heart and life of the Chief Shepherd.

The "shepherding function" in church leadership jargon tends to focus on the care of individuals. Certainly spiritual leaders can never diminish the value or ignore individuals, not when they have the model of their Good Shepherd leaving the ninety-nine to go and find the wandering one. However, the emphasis often missing is on the *flock, not the individual sheep.* The guidance and protection of actual "church" shepherds requires as strong an emphasis on "flock-focus," on the corporate whole, as upon individual-focus.

Many meetings of pastors and lay leaders purport to be "flock-focused." I have spent countless hours in board and committee meetings. We accomplished some things at these meetings, some strategies and plans moved forward, some objectives were set and met, some relationships were strengthened and some tested. However, the best leadership my lay leaders and I gave to our church was to work through its history and address the things God had been trying to teach us over the years. When those people in church leadership understood and participated in that process, together we helped free the church from the limits of its history. That work of corporate leadership led to a spiritual renewal in our church. Jesus, speaking to our church as He did to the seven churches in Revelation, kept addressing those things He knew were corporately keeping us from what He wanted us to be. It is the good work, the unique challenge, of spiritual leadership—pastors, elders, and deacons—to discern and address these things.

Many members can do the other forms of work and ministry around a church, but *only appointed spiritual leaders in the congregation can do this work.* Indeed if they do not do it, no one else can. This is what their spiritual authority within a church equips them to do.

God tells us His blueprint for authority in Romans 13:1-7. God has appointed *all authority* for corporate welfare and empowered it to provide for, protect, praise and punish the people under it. We know that "the authorities" do not always act as God has designed; nevertheless God has a blueprint. Those having spiritual authority in the church, above all others, should be aware of that divine blueprint.

The uniqueness of mediatorial authority. There is one dimension to the blueprint not often recognized because it is fairly foreign to our thinking: the *mediatorial or representative dimension* to authority. It is quite remarkable. The kings and priests in the Old Testament stood *for their people* before God. God charged the kings of Israel with upholding and enforcing the legal statutes of the Mosaic covenant. You cannot read the history of these kings without one striking fact becoming clear: As the heart of the king went, so went the hearts of the people for the most part (with some obvious exceptions). However, God dealt with the "organization" or country based primarily on the actions and attitudes of the king. The king thus "stood" for the rest of the country before God. He was their mediatorial "head." When the king's heart was good, he led the country in obedience to God's commands. Under such kings as Josiah or Hezekiah, God blessed and delivered the people. When a king's heart was evil, he led the people in disobedience to God's commands. Under such kings as Manasseh or Ahab, the people and the country experienced judgments as promised in Deuteronomy.

The high priest likewise stood mediatorially on behalf of the congregation before God in religious things. Our theologies term this "federal headship." On Yom Kippur he would enter the Holy of Holies on behalf of the people—one man on behalf of all—and offer a sacrifice to cover the sins of the congregation of Israel. Jesus, by the offer of His sacrifice, is the single mediator between God and all humans when it comes to eternal salvation (1 Tim. 2:5; Heb. 10:1-18). As the Second Adam, He could stand for all humans by His death and righteous life (Romans 5:15-19). As the King of kings and Lord of lords, He has all authority (Matt. 28:19). His roles as Savior of the world and as Absolute Authority over humankind are linked (Phil. 2:5-11; Hebrews 1:3-4). Jesus combines the role of Priest and King—religious and governmental authority—according to the order of Melchizedek (Heb. 7). Paul accurately says of Jesus that God "gave Him to be head over all things to the church." Jesus could offer what He offered because of who He is.

Pastors and spiritual leadership in the local church now combine both governmental and religious functions within the church. *All believers are royal (kingly) priests* (1 Pet. 2:9,10). Let no one misconstrue that I hold to anything else but that doctrine deeply rooted in the Reformation. Martin Luther rightly and righteously reacted to the spiritual inferiority/superiority division that existed in his day between "laity and clergy." However, I also believe the Reformation church *overreacted*. Even in the priesthood of the Old Testament there were orders, levels and degrees that distinguished the work of the priests. God designed these divisions to be based, not on superiority, but on role and function.

The point is this: Those in spiritual leadership *can* represent the corporate body and speak for them before God and men, even as a husband can as head of his family. With this mediatorial authority (as with all authority) comes accountability (Heb.13:17). Spiritual leaders manage/ govern the church as the household of God (1 Tim. 3:5) and as believer "chief priests" they lead the congregation in intercession and operate as shepherds on their behalf (1 Tim. 2:1-3; Acts 20:28).

Through the ages, those in spiritual leadership have done damage by taking more authority unto themselves than God intended. They have elevated themselves with titles and positions that divide them from the flock rather than unite them to it as mediatorial authority does (Matthew 23:1-7). The tendency is to become "locked" in a polarized relationship with the congregation that manifests itself in an "us-them" attitude common with church staff and church Boards. It is as the "Man Christ Jesus" that Jesus operates as the Mediator between God and man (1 Tim. 2:5). *His oneness with us is the basis for His mediatorial authority over us.* The reason for this is simple: If He were not one with us, He could not stand for us. It is the oneness the pastor and spiritual leaders have with the congregation that is the basis for their mediatorial authority. As soon as they adopt an "us-them" attitude, they cease to be effective in mediatorial ministry.

The use of mediatorial authority. What should one do with mediatorial authority? I believe its unique use is in the *corporate* leadership I have described. This in no way implies that the individuals in the corporate body cease to be responsible for their choices. When the leadership discovers the things Jesus has been communicating to the church, they are in the role and position *to do something about it*. They can act on behalf of the congregation and deal with the corporate issues and address historical problems. These may entail wounds created by former pastors, boards, splits, power plays, doctrinal problems, unresolved corporate conflicts or moral issues. The problems may go back generations. All of them directly impact the heart of a church. All of them are the kinds of things Jesus addresses in Revelation 2 and 3.

The apostle Paul calls the leaders of the church to this kind of function. In a little practiced part of the New Testament, the apostle describes mediatorial church leadership in terms of its ability to judge the affairs of church life.

If any of you has a dispute with another, dare he take it before the ungodly for judgment instead of before the saints? Do you not know that the saints will judge the world? And if you are to judge the world, are you not competent to judge trivial cases? Do you not know that we will judge angels? How much more the things of this life! Therefore, if you have disputes about such matters, appoint as judges even men of little account in the church! I say this to shame you. Is it possible that there is nobody among you wise enough to judge a dispute between believers? But instead, one brother goes to law against another—and this in front of unbelievers! (1 Cor. 6:1-6, NIV)

Paul sarcastically relates that even appointing believers to judge who are "of little account" is better than going before unbelievers. Novice Christians are better equipped to judge the conflicts within the Corinthian church than any outsider.

However, Paul's sarcastic tone here should not diminish the significance of what he says to his target audience—church leadership. They are the "wise" ones, competent and capable to judge the affairs of the church, particularly the conflicts between believers. Would there be any conflict in the church, no matter how large or how old, that wise appointed leaders could not judge and to which they could not discern a solution? Indeed such judging is ministry preparation for the next world.

To learn to exercise such judgment is good leadership. This is the kind of leadership that makes a powerful difference. This is the kind of leadership that changes unhealthy or destructive patterns in a church. Along with the important tasks of communicating biblical values and establishing a vision and strategy for the church I believe dealing with corporate "heart" problems is the work of its mediatorial leadership. If a church's leadership does not do these things, there is no one else to be found who can do them.

Summary. Spiritual authority is unique in nature and power. A key aspect of this God-given authority is a spiritual leader's ability to stand as a mediator on behalf of those over whom he has charge. This "mediatorial authority" enables spiritual leaders, both pastoral and lay leaders, to act on behalf of the congregation to "fix" things at a corporate level. Nevertheless, even the New Testament church leaders often failed to exercise this authority. To learn to use it wisely is the good work of leadership.

Chapter 4

THE HEART OF MATTERS

Churches are like individual believers. They all have spiritual journeys within their culture—a spiritual birth, initial exciting growth, temptations and challenges, ruts and routines. They make choices along the way related to their spiritual values and modes of operation. Jesus has been sending a message *to every local church* as unique as the ones in Revelation 2 and 3. Those seven local churches were just miles apart from each other, yet each one had its own unique set of issues and problems. The challenge to each one was "he who has ears to hear, let him hear." Somehow the church leadership has to figure out what God has been trying to teach the corporate body of the local church. Then it can use its God-given ability to judge how best to solve the corporate problem.

As a part of a course I teach on Revelation, my students write a "Revelation-type" letter from Jesus to their local church. I love the creative responses. I wonder if some of them are not right-on, like "To Forest City Church, He who was not born yesterday says this: I know your works, that you have your doctrines straight and your loves twisted." I love it! What would you say in such a letter to your church? What would be the heart of the matter between Jesus and your faith community?

The need to get at the root. Getting to the root of your church's problems and struggles requires a review of your church's spiritual journey. Most of us (if not all) can look back on our personal spiritual journeys and know what God was trying to teach us. Time gives us perspective. We know how God used pain and trials to open our eyes to things we needed to get right. *We know there were times when God would not let us go any farther until we dealt with something.* That became the key issue, the heart of the matter to God. It did not matter what else we had going, what ministries we were involved in, God would not let us progress spiritually until we addressed this key issue.

Is it possible churches are the same? I believe they are. If there are inexplicable problems in the present, they doubtless are rooted in the soil of your church's history. Perhaps your church is filled with rancor. Was it always this way? It may seem like it. As bitterness is a root which, "springing up, causes trouble and defiles many" (Heb. 12:15), the corporate bitterness or suspicion defiling your congregation now was planted as a seed in your church's heart in times past.

Does your church have a reputation for running down or burning out its pastors? Does it have a pattern of a six month honeymoon with a new pastor, before the onset of gossip begins about him or his family for the next six months, growing dissatisfaction with the preaching or his failure to visit or evangelize or whatever people think he should be doing for the next six months, and finally a concerted effort to make life so miserable for the final six months that he leaves? Then they get a new pastor to do it all again. If it's not so predictable a pattern as this, is there something else that is just as destructive to the health of spiritual leadership—a dominant family that always gets its way, a history of immorality among board members or musicians, the burning out of associate staff?

If you are a pastor reading this book and have been in your church more than a year, chances are you have run into something rotten. Let me ask you, do you know why the man before you left? You may have heard the people in the church explain it, and you may even have talked to the former pastor before you took the call to the church, but did you really probe to understand what, if anything, went wrong? If two pastors left in quick succession, what happened? There may be reasonable explanations that have nothing to do with the church, but it sure would raise the alarm for me until I found out why.

Once you understand that such problems and patterns get rooted in the church family the same way they have gotten rooted in your own family, you can begin to address them. It takes courage, and just because you or the church leadership starts to address them is no guarantee that the congregation will follow. The people of God have always made such enterprises iffy at best. Some congregations can prefer the dysfunctional *status quo* (Latin for "the mess we are in") the same as families, and resist all efforts to change. God will keep them in pain until they do.

The tendency to focus on superficialities. It is not at all uncommon for churches and church leaders to focus on superficial problems with superficial solutions. Almost always this effort is either individually or program focused. For all the energy poured into trying to fix things, nothing much changes. The heart of the church has not changed.

I faced the challenge of trying to understand and address a string of failed leadership initiatives in our church (I will explain in more detail next chapter). I wanted to launch an initiative that would work, so I tackled a long list of superficial issues—timing, communication, preparation for launch, developing a team, etc.—that I thought would ensure success, thinking these were the reasons the former initiatives failed. I was wrong. They were not the heart of the matter. Until we dealt with the heart of the matter, initiatives of any significant kind were doomed.

I counseled briefly with a church where there had been two successive pastors who had experienced some painful things at the hands of certain individuals in the congregation. One pastor had internalized the conflict, got sick and left. The second pastor became combative, defensive, and left. That pastor was still hurting and enraged by the way that he was treated when I met him a year later. "The only way I will talk to those people again is if they offer a formal apology," he told me. As I heard the stories from both the elders and this former pastor, it became clear that they had established a destructive pattern. The pain of it had a lasting impact on the second pastor. He was not sure he ever wanted to take another church ministry.

I sought to bring the parties together in reconciliation, a major change in the status quo. The status quo demanded that the pastors remain estranged, and that the congregation and Board remain distrustful of pastors. They had done nothing about the instigators. Now they were about to call a new pastor. If there were ever a time to work this out, it was before that new man came. During lunch with several elders, they described to me the attempt to ensure it would not happen by the *kind* of man they called. This is a common congregational plan. They believe the personality of the previous pastor (in this case combative) is the problem, so they attempt to find someone with a very different personality. They forget they also did that before they called the combative pastor.

"You guys *have* to be scared to death," I said. "You know and I know that you cannot ensure that the exact same things will not happen again. Nothing has changed."

They were truthful. "We are scared, but we just can not bring ourselves to do what is necessary to reconcile with the previous pastor." So you have a scared leadership and probably a scared church. Fear creates reactivity and reactivity reinforces unhealthy patterns. They will overcompensate and avoid dealing with stuff they should. They are afraid it will blow up, or become suspicious and think "Oh no, here we go again," at the first sign of trouble. *The very things they do to prevent trouble will create it.*

They called their new man, who, interestingly, did not talk to the previous pastor before taking the position. I pray things are different, but not much has occurred to change the pattern. How can the Boards and congregation trust this new man? Just because he is a different personality? He is a pastor, and at the first hint of anything similar to the previous administration they will become fearful. He will see or sense this reaction and wonder, "Where on earth did *this* come from?" It will probably stimulate some sort of reactivity in him (depending on his own history), and the cycle begins all over. The really painful thing is that there is apt to be another pastoral casualty before long.

It is not enough to deal with superficialities like personality (which is only superficial in this instance). One sees this in serial divorces. Personalities are interchangeable while nothing changes in the pattern of relating. It did not matter what my wife's personality was. I feared feminine anger and reacted any time I saw a flash of it. There might be more anger, there might be less, but my reaction was the same. That was the heart of the matter, and not much would change until I dealt with it. *Pastors and church leadership have to get to this "heart of the matter" in their church.*

Another illustration will help. I was a friend with several pastors who came and went at a nearby church. This church, planted in the early 70's when body life and *koinonia* were the current trends (the church's color motif was orange and purple), was rooted in a cycle of calling entrepreneurial pastors (like their first pastor) to do modern, relevant outreach then resisting all their efforts. I watched some really fine men go through this ministry and leave in utter frustration and with a fair amount of rancor. Someone had to address this pattern of behavior rooted in the church's history, otherwise it was unlikely much would change. This destructive pattern of reactivity grew with each successive pastor. The pastors, for their part, felt betrayed. They saw the rules regarding their call to that church change midstream. So they either became more reactive to churches that called them or went out and started their own churches to avoid having to deal with traditional ministries, all of which seemed treacherous.

Wobbling plates are not the heart of the matter. The man who mentored me compared pastors to the plate spinners at a carnival. I would add to the image by dressing them in firefighter's garb holding a lightning rod in one hand. While keeping all the plates of ministry spinning, they have to put out all the brush fires around them that a spiritual arsonist (Satan) is constantly setting. Meanwhile they hold the lightning rod to discharge the normal tensions, frustrations and anger that floats like static electricity in any community of people living in close proximity and learning to get along.

This laughable, frenetic image is too true for the modern pastor. The problem is with what we often perceive as "the real problem" in the church. Many times a wobbling plate is seen as the heart of the matter. Every church has wobbling plates. Pastors will never escape the ministry of dealing with the constant challenges of understaffed ministries essential for the church's function. Wobbling plates include the seniors' ministry that the 80 seniors in your church want but no one wants to lead or the fact that you never can get enough people for your nursery (I have never been in a church that *did not* have announcements about needing nursery workers in their bulletins).

When pastors are under stress, these minor irritants become major issues. Often they can be the proverbial straw that breaks the camel's back, especially if a senior calls to complain or a harried nursery worker levels a blast at the pastor on the way out of church. Stress causes us to lose perspective on what is important, and small problems grow large. I have known pastors who are losing perspective, to get up and yell at their congregations about the lack of volunteers in the nursery. I know how that feels. I even heard of one pastor who got up and said, "We don't have enough nursery workers today, so I am going to the nursery to help. One of you can preach!" and off the platform he marched.

The seniors and the nursery are important, but they are not the heart of the matter. The *patterns that create such stress in the pastor are at the heart of the matter*. The perpetual wobbling plate of nursery volunteerism could not do that by itself. It is an illusion to believe that solving the nursery or seniors problems will change what is going on in the heart of the church.

Brush fires are not the heart of the matter. Pastors are constantly dousing the many brush fires in their church because Satan is constantly setting fires. Brush fires range from the hurt feelings of the latest soloist (someone complained that her music was too loud), to the plaster bust of Gene Simmons of K.I.S.S. the youth found in a treasure hunt that they have now ensconced outside their room at the church, which, of course (Satan arranges this), is right next to the Galilean Sunday School class of 70 year-olds.

Brush fires include the twenty-page epistle correcting the pastor's view of the Tribulation (by producing one itself), his view of the role of women, his view of divorce and remarriage, his view of home schooling, his view of whatever. They include the ongoing conflict between the church secretary and the church youth pastor who never tells her where he is going or when he will be back. They seldom involve large groups of people, but can spread if not tended and doused.

Just when the pastor thinks he has the fires all extinguished, three more spring to life. Yet as much attention and energy as they require, brush fires are not the real problem in most churches. Just dousing them will never change the heart of the church.

Lightning rods are not the heart of the matter. Lightning rods are "anger attractors" in church ministry. They involve people who have general, non-specific unhappiness and will focus the energy of their gripe in corporate conflict. Like a buildup of static electricity in the atmosphere, growing or residual anger and frustration in a congregation will seek lightning rods for discharge. Some common lightning rods are worship styles (contemporary vs. traditional), changes in service times, pastoral personality, seeker or non-seeker services, or styles of preaching or particular messages which create an "issue" in the church. Lightning rods create hot spots where fires smolder and are potentially explosive. Both the potential to explode and the explosive reactions themselves are what I call "sinful reactivity." Some stimulus sets off a reaction far greater than the stimulus warrants. When a pastor holds a lightning rod (and he usually does), he and his ministry are considered a hot spot and produce sinful reactions.

Have you ever been burned by such a discharge of congregational anger? Sometimes we see the thunderheads building; sometimes it catches us completely unawares. A business meeting blindsided me once. In my second ministry we faced difficult times as we worked to implement our vision. Because of the increased leadership demands I had delegated the Wednesday prayer meeting to an associate who wanted more opportunities to teach. I also set up a rotating schedule of who spoke on Sunday nights so I did not have to do all of them. Historically, only the senior pastor did these things.

All the changes made some of our older saints unhappy but they were uncertain about how to express that unhappiness. Static electricity was building in the atmosphere. The lightning struck at a church business meeting. One of the senior "pillars" of the church stood and read a letter "on behalf of many people who had talked to him." In it he complained about the changes in the church, particularly the fact that the church now had a "part-time senior pastor." My wife and I sat there like someone had socked us in the solar plexus.

The heart of the matter for our church became evident in what happened next. No one stood to speak on our behalf. Our church's core issue was its fear and avoidance of conflict. It was an ongoing pattern based on its painful history. The church did not have a healthy way of handling conflict. Neither did I. The result was a real toxic mixture.

When the heart of the matter is evident and starts to impact relationships within the corporate body, the pastor and church experience powerful pain, the kind of pain that sends people running for emotional cover or for emotional weaponry. They fail to realize that such pain is God's megaphone to call them away from such destructive patterns.

Something bad may be happening in your church. It may be a history of running off pastors or of tolerating immorality among its board members. Maybe long-term conflicts never get resolved. The demands of pastoral ministry often keep a pastor focused on superficial problems. To change things, the pastor must be willing to explore the real sources of his own pain as well as the church's pain.

Chapter 5

CORPORATE AND LEADERSHIP PAIN: THE MEGAPHONE OF GOD

How does God send messages to His local churches? How does He communicate that something is wrong?

How does a body usually know something is wrong? It experiences pain. Yet how often we miss this simple question and answer in a leadership assessment of a church's corporate history. If there is something wrong in the heart of your church, it will express itself in a variety of ways. My story illustrates how this happens.

Manifestations of pain. I bumped–actually, I ran—headlong into manifestations of corporate pain in my previous ministry. I remember vividly the three business meetings on consecutive Sundays required to pass a church budget. The congregation was highly suspicious of the things the board recommended in this budget. It made no sense to me, given the makeup of the board. Why were people acting this way? I did not understand it at the time, but I was witnessing an expression of corporate pain.

You can guess how I responded to this conflict. I threw myself into the middle and stretched out my hands in martyrdom to soak up the anger between the board and the congregation. At the subsequent meetings, I read two letters seeking conciliation by placating the congregation. The fact that I was getting in the way only made them angrier.

The congregation's mistrust and suspicion toward the board did not appear to be coming from an individual or even a small group. It was in the air. That became apparent when I had the board members stand, called out their names one by one, and asked the congregation, "Which one of these men don't you trust? Point him out." No one said a word. The truth was that the board was made up of godly men and the congregation knew it. However, the attitude of mistrust for the whole board remained. Why? There was something going on in the heart of my church and I was ignorant of it.

I should have recognized it. When I came to the church to candidate, someone used a phrase that should have been my first clue: "Our church does not know what it wants to be when it grows up." The church was 29 years old when I arrived! Consider parents who have a 29-year-old direction-less child still living at home. Rather than pity them, I heard the statement as a cry for a vision, a mission, and a strategy dynamic enough to inspire people. I would draw on my strengths and experiences from my former ministry. What I should have detected was an identity problem. There was something blocking this church's ability to know who it was and why it existed.

As I met with two search committee members during my candidacy, I told them how impressed I was by the significant strategies the boards of the church had developed. They had constructed—on paper—a wonderful disci-pleship strategy, a lay counseling strategy, a prayer ministry strategy. They had come up with a dynamic "unleashing your church" strategy before Frank Tillipaugh published his book. They had sent these documents to me before-hand. I remember sitting in a restaurant with the two search committee members and asking innocently, "How much of this has been implemented?" They just looked at each other and blushed.

"Well, ah . . .you see, we haven't been as successful at implementing these initiatives as we have been at developing them," one admitted.

"Yes, but," the other said brightly, "that's what we want our new pastor to help us to do."

I bet you pastors love that! You are either laughing or crying or both. You may be shaking your head and thinking, "You poor, ignorant sap."

Hindsight is lasic clear. I should have heard klaxons. There was some sort of disconnect between the leadership's ideas and initiatives, and its ability to lead the congregation to implement them. It was a clear manifestation of congregational pain, this time experienced by the board and former pastor. However, my ego and self-confidence—and a clear call from God to go and learn the painful lessons that I now share with you (though God wisely never puts it that way to us)—led me to accept the position. I felt that I could help them get unstuck.

Entering a church with a history. It was a church with a glorious past. The old-timers recalled the time in the late 60s to the early 70s when they were the only church in Canada operating as a training center for Evangelism Explosion. People came from all over Canada and the north-eastern U.S. for training in evangelism. They canvassed the neighborhoods surrounding the church and shared the gospel. People came to Christ by the dozens, and the church grew to 500+ in attendance under the leadership of its founding pastor. It came to be one of the larger evangelical churches in Canada at that time. But in 1975 they had a horrific split. When the smoke cleared and the founding pastor left, the church shrunk to about 100. The second pastor, a solid man, rebuilt the ministry and the attendance grew again to about 350. Facing the uphill struggle to implement anything, he had left discouraged.

Then I arrived. I determined to be cautious. I spent, not just one, but two years "sitting by the well" and listening to people before I began to outline a vision and strategy. I wanted it to fit our context and culture and not parrot what someone else was doing. I wanted to build a team. I felt that non-implemented initiatives had been presented so many times the congregation was jaundiced about initiatives in general; I had to make certain that when we moved forward, we were ready and credible.

The birth of a vision. Finally, early in my third year, I had lunch with the former youth pastor. He mentioned in passing, "Wouldn't it be great if we could start daughter churches that would share ministry resources with the mother church? Ministry resources always seem to be the problem. It's difficult for a church plant that only has a few teenagers for a youth ministry to attract people who have teens and want a ministry for them."

That passing comment planted the seed of a vision in me. In the next year we forged an exciting vision for multiple "daughter" congregations under the umbrella of one church, each congregation with its own pastor and board, but in close proximity to each other so that they could share ministry resources together. Each congregation would target a different group in our community with pastors and staff chosen with skills to reach that group of people. Living in an urban, highly multicultural area, this vision for multiple congregations reaching different people groups but sharing resources made so much sense. Land was at a premium and our church was land-locked so there was no way to grow except move or multiply. I gathered a team and we formulated a vision for multiplication of congregations. We called it both the 20/20 vision—twenty congregations by the year 2020 (about 1 per year out of our church)—and "the Matrix strategy" (long before the movie of the same name). Matrix is from the Latin *mater* or mother. A "matrix" was actually an animal used for breeding and that is what we wanted the mother church to become.

Little did I know that the vision was doomed from the beginning because of what had happened fifteen years before when the church split. However, this fatal flaw wasn't discernable at first. We developed a complicated new constitution for the church allowing for multiple congregations while we prayed and pursued the right target group for the first congregation.

The presentation of the vision and the early stages went as most visions do: some excitement, some wait-and-see, some naysayers. Nevertheless, the leadership was committed and ready, committees were up and running, the new constitution voted on and passed. A group of pioneers gathered to make up the core of the second congregation and we were off. In short order we had called a pastor to lead this second congregation whose goal was to reach the unchurched parents of the kids in our large youth ministry.

Pain amplification. Meanwhile, in the mother congregation I pastored, things were not going smoothly. Because many of our young people joined the more contemporary second congregation, members were accusing it of "splitting families." The choir became a huge arena for malcontents. They would sit behind me and scowl through the music portion of the worship service. A pastor once told me that he thought when Satan fell from heaven, he fell into the choir loft. I would not have argued at that point. I kept trying to absorb this conflict, hoping it would shrink or disappear. I believed that once the second congregation grew and established itself, once some people came to Christ and were publicly baptized, once some time passed and everyone got used to the idea, everything would calm down.

The second congregation did grow. In nine months it grew to about 70 people. Almost viable, but not quite. The choir had gotten so horrible I canceled it. No more choir. Talk about a storm of anger! I was furiously trying to absorb the conflict now, but it was way over my head. Not surprisingly, the second congregation began to have conflicts of various kinds (like mother, like child). Eventually the pastor resigned, but not before blasting me for implementing such a stupid idea that only fed my ego.

The wheels came off. In three years we went from conception of the vision to its implementation and growth, to its annihilation. It was not pretty. Five years into my ministry and I faced a huge failure as a leader. I had no clue what to do about it. I figured my ministry there was over. Who would follow my leadership now? What initiative could I possibly bring to this church?

So once again the congregation and leadership were in major pain. Jesus was speaking to His church, telling us something was very wrong. He was speaking to me about the way I handle conflict. We—the congregation and I—still did not know how to listen to Him.

What could I learn from this fiasco? I asked the superintendent of our church association to do a thorough analysis of what went wrong and to submit a report to the board and me. The results didn't make me feel better.

The superintendent concluded that I did not cause the problem and probably could not have prevented the failure. My vision for the church was shattered. I still cannot think about it without pain.

Time to leave? I assumed my ministry in this church was over, and nothing remained but to send out my rèsumÈ and move. But God did not open any doors. Finally a church in New Jersey that sounded like a possibility contacted us. We arranged to candidate on the way back from our vacation. All during that vacation my wife experienced a strange set of symptoms: sleeplessness, heart palpitations, shortness of breath and heart pain. We attributed it to the stress of candidating. When we arrived back home, the symptoms increased. My wife went to the doctor and discovered she had a thyroid problem and a major heart blockage. Within the month she had life saving open-heart surgery. We were not going anywhere. At that time I knew we could not reenter the States and get insurance (they have changed the laws since then), but no opportunities were opening in Canada either.

At the emotional level I felt that God did not just shut the door for me to leave—He slammed it! I was more than a little angry with Him. I had no clue what to do with a degenerating, increasingly conflictual ministry. How conflictual? I had a couple—former choir members who were hard of hearing—who used to make loud comments to each other while I was preaching. "Where did he get *that* from? I don't see *that* in the text." "I do not believe what he is saying, do you?" "That's just flat out wrong!" Other church members were concerned enough to fill up the pews around this couple so that a visitor couldn't sit within earshot.

My role of taking blame for everything was killing me. I had a very sick wife. I felt totally powerless to change my circumstances. I understand why someone would read the want ads with longing and the obituaries with envy. Powerlessness does that. If pain is God's megaphone, He could not have spoken much louder to me.

I began to invest my energy in counseling. I had done some counseling, but not much. Now I focused on it. Counseling was the only ministry task that I felt positive about. Interestingly, this is exactly what the founding pastor of the church had done as things began to fall apart for him.

Time to do something different? One day I got a phone call from one of the members complaining about something. It was no worse than usual, but I was at the end of my tether and I cracked. I came home early and told my wife I had to do something else with my life. I simply could not do pastoral ministry any more. The next day I took my first "mental health day" in ministry. I went to the library and checked on degree programs for counseling training.

I am convinced two things saved my life at this time. First, God mercifully led me into a prayer group of local pastors. At that time a Billy Graham Crusade in Toronto had hooked pastors together for prayer who lived in the same locale. I know that God sustained me through the prayers of these warriors, several of them as battle-scarred as I was. They listened sympathetically to my whining and woes, and prayed for me from their hearts. I cannot express how significant such a support group was to a hurting pastor.

The second thing that saved me was that I found a Doctor of Ministry program in Marriage and Family Therapy. I headed off to get a second doctorate, one I hoped would give me a viable alternative to pastoral ministry. I was already educated beyond my intelligence so what was another degree? Little did I know the impact it would have.

Learning about the four quadrants. Two thirds of the way through that program I learned about the four quadrants (Birth Family, Marriage and Present Family, Congregational Family and God's Child) and their influence on each other. I also began to probe in depth my own family history. This is where (as I shared earlier) I joined my siblings at a condo in the mountains. I recorded the memories of elderly members of my family. Slowly I filled in the picture and grasped the nature of the generational patterns being passed along. I realized that the roles I chose when in conflict were burning me out as they had burned out my father before me. With the Spirit's encouragement and enablement I addressed the unhealthy patterns in my marriage and experienced a new level of intimacy.

I had worked on my marriage and now turned to the congregational family. "If this worked in my marriage, could it possibly work for me in dealing with my conflicts in the church?" I wondered. I had nothing to lose at this point. I still aimed to leave and open a counseling center after I got my degree. All they could do was fire me. So I committed myself again into the hands of Christ and entered that dysfunctional congregational climate one Sunday morning determined to raise no barriers, to hide behind no defenses or distance myself emotionally, to be completely "present" with those people.

Whoa! Not only did I experience a profound connection with them, I felt the *presence of God* like I never had before in our worship. Something changed there that was unexpected. I had finally begun to address what Jesus had been talking to me about for a long time. My ongoing pain and turmoil proved that He was connecting to me. This newfound intimacy in all my relationships was the reward for obedience and faith. The quadrants are intricately connected.

The truth I discovered here was profound. I had changed, but the congregation had not. I had changed, but my wife had not. Both these changes had a deep impact on the way I related, on the safety and freedom I felt. *I was not powerless!* It was then that it struck me—*what if the church's problems, like my own, were rooted in its history*? I suspected they were, but I was not sure how to approach it. However, I was determined to try.

Chapter 6

THE GOOD, THE BAD, AND THE UGLY: YOUR CHURCH'S SPIRITUAL JOURNEY

If I were sitting face to face with you right now and I asked you, "Do you think the history of your church might have something to do with some of the painful things you are experiencing right now?" my guess is that you would answer, "Probably." "Oh yeah, they have done this before."

As our teenagers would say, "Like, duh." If you are anything like I am, the thought of my struggles having its roots in the church's history simply never occurred to me, at least as something I could help heal. It was a fatalistic thought: "They are doing the same things to me that they did to the previous guy." Moreover I considered such history irrelevant. "That was then, this is now. How can talking about something that happened twenty-two years before help anything in this church now?" The question was about to be answered.

Paralleling the personal journey. The process I followed with the church took its direction from my personal journey. If you have done that historical groundwork, you will be better equipped to lead the church. You do not have to do it, but it is wise. You will be convicted by the part history plays in present relationships. If you trust God and are courageous enough to make changes in some of your roles, draw Scriptural boundaries, and take appropriate responsibility, then you will recognize God's power to heal your heart. By healing many of your relationships, He will set you free from things that have bound you.

The key is to relive the experiences of the church's spiritual journey. Climb into the heads and hearts of the founders. Seek the divine directions your church followed when Christ started your church. His purposes were revealed to the founders through their calling, their burden and their vision in early days. Probably many things were accomplished when the church was young and excitement was high. Dig up archives either in the church files or the files of previous pastors or self-appointed church historians (every church seems to have them). Pictures from that time will help jog memories too.

Who should be there? Though the temptation will be strong, if you are a pastor, do not take this journey into your church's history alone. You want *lots of company* at the leadership level. You want some charter members if they are alive. So much of this journey will be about storytelling. I told our church leadership I wanted them to teach me everything about the church, beginning with how it got started. As we approached our fortieth anniversary as a church, I wanted us to reflect on the lessons God had taught our church in the past to equip us to lead it to its next level. Given the fiascoes we had experienced, we needed some reflection to know how to lead us forward. The leadership knew this was true.

Consider inviting some "special guests." These special guests will be key figures from the time period you are focusing on. Some will be members within the church, and others could be people who no longer attend your church. You will need the approval of your leaders to invite them. (It could be a nasty surprise—one you do not want—if you invite unapproved people.) After that approval, contact and brief these guests—they need to know exactly what to expect, and what you expect of them. Also ask the church historian to find relevant records and pictures.

Consider inviting a former pastor (if available) or a former staff member from that time if you believe their presence would be positive. The former clergy or staff member's participation may actually benefit them personally through closure on some issues in their own life and ministry. However, think carefully. This type of reunion is also a risk. The ground rules would have to be agreed upon beforehand. Complete honesty would be the primary requirement. There is also a risk that the former leader's presence might intimidate the lay leaders. There is also a risk that this guest might try to control the agenda. If, however, you put this book in his hand and he reads it, he may become a willing participant. The hope is that everyone will benefit from his participation.

How long will it take? This type of healing journey should be arranged and conducted over a weekend or perhaps a series of weekends a month apart. I naively thought we could do it in one weekend. We needed three and by the time our third retreat was over, everyone was weary. I recommend that you plan for three weekends. That allows you time to process and publish information among the group, making any additions as they come to light. Storytelling takes time and processing the stories takes longer. The older your church is, the longer it will take. The more things that have happened, the longer it will take. If your church is ten years old and had just one pastor, it might not take so long. If it is ten years old, had one split and four pastors, it will take longer.

THE ATTITUDES FOR THE JOURNEY

There are several attitudes you want to carry into this journey that will ensure a healthy result.

Determine to be positive. If your spirit is bitter and you want to rub the church's nose in some of its manure, you are not ready to lead this journey. Do not make your sole purpose to dig for skeletons (though you will probably find plenty). Do not say or think, "I am on a crusade to clean up this pig sty!" Your purpose is to discern God-given lessons. As you journey together, the blessings and grace of God will astonish all of you.

Expect resistance. As soon as the talk begins to revolve around some of the painful times in the church's history, you will see reactions associated with denial. "Why are we talking about this negative stuff?" "Christ has led us on from there; we do not want to go back." My favorite misapplication of Scripture in this context is, "Aren't we supposed to ëforget what lies behind and reach forward to what lies ahead?'" Be ready for this. Don't react as if they are trying to defeat your personal purposes. Go back and help everyone to focus on what God was seeking to teach the church during that painful time. You may need to do a little teaching about pain and suffering from a biblical perspective. People need constant reminders of these truths. There are three ways to approach this sensitive, painful material.

First, ask them to remember the most significant lessons they have learned in their lives. Did they learn them in good times or in bad? Most people have learned their greatest lessons the way that you have—in the painful times. Say something like: "We will examine these painful times by opening up the wounds. The purpose is not to wallow in the painful things but to understand and seek what God was trying to teach our church through them."

Second, remind them of the purpose of trials biblically. James says in 1: 2-4: *"Consider it all joy, my brethren, when you encounter various trials, knowing that the testing of your faith produces endurance. And let endurance have its perfect result, that you may be perfect and complete, lacking in nothing"* (NASV). Trials are gifts from God given to prove our faith and produce endurance that we might become mature believers. James also adds a key phrase, often skipped—that trials come so that we would be "lacking in nothing." God seeks to give us something we lack as we learn endurance through trials. If this is true for trials as individuals, the same would be true for church trials. Ask each other "What did God want to give our church from this painful time?"

Another key passage to consider is Romans 5:2-4. Paul says, *And not only this, but we also exult in our tribulations, knowing that tribulation brings about perseverance; and perseverance, proven character; and proven character, hope; and hope does not disappoint, because the love of God has been poured out within our hearts through the Holy Spirit who was given to us* (NASV). The words "brings about" used here describe a digging process to remove something buried, like mining for jewels. As Paul Billheimer wrote in *Destined for the Throne,* too many of us have "wasted our sorrows." We have not let them dig out what God intended to mine out of our lives. Again, what is true individually is also true corporately. Once more ask, "What did God seek to mine out of our congregation through this church split, through this doctrinal controversy, through the former pastor's adulterous affair? Have God's purposes been accomplished?"

Third, let people know that this is "for you and the younger generation to understand exactly what went on." The prophet Joel knew that the tragedies of Israel's history and the lessons associated with their pain needed to be told and retold to the following generations. Joel 1:2-4 says, *Hear this, O elders, and listen, all inhabitants of the land. Has anything like this happened in your days or in your fathers' days? Tell your sons about it, and let your sons tell their sons, and their sons the next generation. What the gnawing locust has left, the swarming locust has eaten; and what the swarming locust has left, the creeping locust has eaten; and what the creeping locust has left, the stripping locust has eaten* (NASV). What Joel and Israel experienced as a locust plague had spiritual implications that every generation needed to learn.

You do not want the old adage, "History teaches that men learn nothing from history," to be true of your church. You want to learn from the painful things of the past so the church doesn't repeat them. You are not digging up these painful memories to wallow in them. You want to hear the whole story in order to learn what God wanted to teach your church.

Draw a time-line map of your church's journey. You want to divide your church's journey into stages. Every journey has stages and "waypoints," moments when there are shifts in direction. Let the leadership decide these turning points. Sometimes waypoints occur around pastors and their comings and goings (less so if the church has had a frequent turnover of pastors). Sometimes major shifts in direction occur around key events and tragedies— a split, a fire, a revival, the tragic death of a key member, or moving locations.

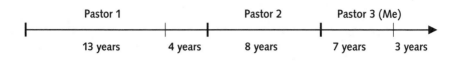

Figure 1

Our timeline looked like this (see Figure 1). Our church had three pastors in 38 years, so the leadership decided there were three major divisions around these pastorates. Within the first pastor's tenure of 17 years, there was a minor division around growth then decline. Within my tenure there was a second minor division due to changes they saw in me (later, as a result of our work and actions, the church went into a renewal which would have been a part of this second division). The gaps in the time line (the tenures only add up to thirty-five) don't include years when the church was without a pastor.

Figure 2 is another example of a timeline for a church that is 19 years old. It's waypoints are based on growth periods and a split.

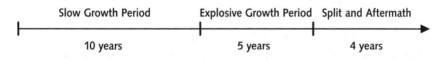

Figure 2

You may divide your timeline up according to the divisions determined as the key waypoints by those in leadership and long-time members of the church.

Chart the rise and fall of attendance over the decades on the timeline. If your church keeps attendance records, this should not be difficult. Our church did not track attendance so we needed to guesstimate. Face it, attendance—especially when it happens in big swings—is a barometer of much of what is happening in the heart of a church. We may not like it, but that is often the case.

As I led our leaders through this process, the attendance graph told its own story and showed the moments of crisis, especially in the ministry of the first pastor. It also signaled trouble in mine.

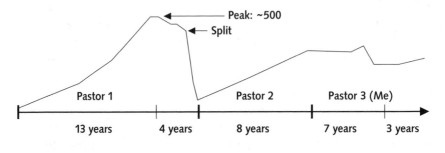

Figure 3

Once you have this general overview of the history, you want to analyze the separate sections, focusing on different aspects of each ministry period. Look at each of these through the lenses Jesus uses to examine the churches of Revelation 2 and 3.

THE START-UP PERIOD

The beginning of every church is unique. Depending upon how old your church is, it is critical to pinpoint the initial impetus for its existence in both historic records and testimony. What was the driving vision responsible for starting the church? Has it changed? What changed it? Was it a church plant? A split? If it was a split, what was the issue that caused the split? Did your church grow from a thriving Bible study? What was in the heart of the founders? Where were the church leaders doctrinally? The answers to these questions provide a perspective on the hopes and dreams of people who invested heavily at the beginning, and could reveal some of the baggage they may have carried into the start of the ministry.

Our church began as the result of a gift. The original owner gave the property to the church to build on with the understanding and stipulation that one quarter of its budget would always go to missions. No one had told me about this commitment when I arrived. It explained why our missions budget was so high. The leadership and members would be in violation of this "ancient covenant" should we ever change it. I could have stumbled into such a violation through sheer ignorance. I believe that many pastors inadvertently and unintentionally violate such ancient boundaries. There are consequences to doing so.

THE BLESSINGS

One of the things that stands out in the letters to the seven churches of Revelation is that Jesus is honest about both the good and the bad. *"I know your works/deeds"* is His refrain, but He is quick to commend them for what they are doing right. As you review your church's history, you want to be careful to do the same. Listen to what Jesus says to the local church in Thyatira: *"I know your deeds, your love and faith, your service and perseverance, and that you are now doing more than you did at first"* (Rev. 2:19 NIV).

Can you remember specific blessings that God has given to your church? Share and record the specific stories from the people gathered for each part of the defined history. You might want to list them on an overhead or blackboard or on a flipchart. I like a flipchart because you can tear off the sheets and hang them on the wall as the story unfolds. What kind of things was God doing? Ask probing questions to help people articulate why they considered each thing a blessing at the time. Were things happening that enabled God to bless this ministry particularly?

In our discussion, the charter members talked about the significance of the Christmas pageants in the early years of our church. God had sent a talented woman to lead these productions, and they drew tremendous crowds. People still spoke of them with fondness thirty years afterward—a sure sign of a divine blessing.

Many times pastors who are seeking to move a church forward are seen as devaluing a glorious past. This especially rubs older people in the congregation the wrong way; they resist him all the more. Working through the historic blessings and celebrating afresh what God has done in your church validates the feelings of old-timers. This affirms that you do value what they treasure; you are not trampling on their pearls. But this exercise will also do something more. God spoke to the church by blessing these things. Hopefully it will help unlock what God was telling the church at that time.

THE CHALLENGES

In Revelation 2 and 3, Jesus also demonstrates that He is fully aware of the challenges each of the seven churches face in their culture and locations. Sometimes the challenge is in the form of outside opposition: *"I know the slander of those who say they are Jews and are not, but are a synagogue of Satan"* (2:9); *"I know where you live—where Satan has his throne. Yet you remain true to my name"* (2:13 NIV).

You need the gathered leaders to talk about some of the challenges the church faced during each period. Challenges are not necessarily conflicts. You will discuss conflicts later. Challenges are those things that required the church to adjust its ministry; challenges require the leadership to lead and show initiative.

Because our church grew so rapidly in the early years, the leadership had to face the challenge of what to do with the growth. Every room in the church was packed with children in Sunday school. Even with the physical limitations of our building, it was a credit to the problem-solving ability of those leaders as they found ways to teach so many and still reach out to more.

Our church was also one of the first in Canada to call a full-time youth pastor. It was a direct response to the growing number of teenagers attending. The pastor and boards were willing to create a ministry without a model. That initiative led to one of the finest youth ministries in the city for decades, a training ground for other youth pastors who came as interns or literally grew up through the ministry.

As you talk about these times, the pastor can affirm many leadership values he may want to encourage once again in a new vision initiative.

THE CONFLICTS

Jesus also addressed conflicts in the seven local churches. Conflicts are as normal in church life as they are in marriage and family life. Conflicts usually revolve around people or issues that require the leaders to confront and resolve something potentially dangerous to the congregation, especially if left unchecked. Jesus describes conflicts that involve problem people and/or dangerous doctrines that were handled appropriately: *"I know that you cannot tolerate wicked men, that you have tested those who claim to be apostles but are not, and have found them false"* (2:2); or inappropriately: *"I have this against you: You tolerate that woman Jezebel, who calls herself a prophetess. By her teaching she misleads my servants into sexual immorality and the eating of food sacrificed to idols. I have given her time to repent of her immorality, but she is unwilling"* (2:20-21). It is crucial for the leadership in your church to identify and talk about conflicts apparent in the church during each period. Needless to say, this may be the most crucial part of the exercise.

Believers in churches often demonize conflict. They view it as the great destroyer of unity when, in fact it is a normal part of the family experience. I once had a man in seminary boast to me that he and his wife had been married five years and had never argued. I was impressed at the time, assuming this meant they had no conflicts. Now I know that his boast actually meant that he, his wife, or both of them were suppressing their conflicts out of a fear of fighting. They assumed marital conflicts meant their relationship was unhealthy.

How we *deal* with conflict is far more important to God than the nature of the conflict. Why? Conflict builds character. The apostle Paul says in 1 Corinthians 11:18-19, *"In the first place, I hear that when you come together as a church, there are divisions among you, and to some extent I believe it. No doubt there have to be differences among you to show which of you have God's approval"* (NIV). The ones with "approved" character emerge in conflict like cream rising to the top. Paul confirms the emergence of approved leaders as proof that conflicts are necessary for God to raise up leaders to lead the congregation.

Your destiny as leaders may be to become "approved" in this way. As you unfold the church's history, a pattern of unresolved conflicts may emerge that remains embedded in the heart of your church. This is a decisive moment where God calls you to demonstrate the character that can lead your church through its conflicts. At this point, you want to catalog some of the issues that caused conflict in each period.

One of the conflicts we uncovered during the first pastor's tenure was the growing emphasis on counseling toward the end of his time with the church. People began to feel that he spent far too much time with troubled people in the congregation and outside it—and not enough time tending to the needs of everyone else. Unwittingly (and astonishingly), I followed the *exact same pattern.*

Another issue toward the end of his tenure was the formation of cliques in the church. There were unmistakable "in" and "out" groups that created a growing resentment on the part of those trapped in the "outs." People perceived the pastor to have favorites, showing partiality to those who were loyal to him. He equated "loyalty" with agreement and if you disagreed, you were considered disloyal to him. In the light of the split that ultimately came, the "outs" were among the members who stayed. It's no surprise that they became extremely sensitive to issues of partiality on the part of subsequent pastors.

The music ministry in general (and the choir specifically) became a hotbed for conflict with the first pastor. Sound familiar? Uncovering this information helped convince our leadership of the importance of what we were doing. The parallels to our present experience were uncanny. The point man for the original conflict was the choir director. His followers were the instrumentalists. Someone told a bitter story that took place right before the split occurred. The pastor asked an individual to bring special music one Sunday. After finishing his song, the man walked off the platform, down the aisle, and right out of the church! He refused to stay for the pastor's sermon. The memories of this unresolved conflict remained in the heart of the church. Could God be allowing these things to repeat themselves?

Another person reported that the second pastor also had major problems with the choir, which reinforced the reality that God might be doing this. The second pastor asked a woman in the church, an outstanding musician, to lead the choir. She did the unthinkable. Seeking to bring some "professionalism" to the choir, she asked each member to audition. The choir went into loud revolt, convincing the pastor that he had to ask the new choir director to step down. The pastor ended up leading the choir, causing pain all the way around! The revelation that *every pastor had major unresolved conflicts with the choir* fascinated our leaders.

The final festering conflict we uncovered revolved around the way the first pastor related to the lay leaders. He once boasted "I work my board members *hard*. They are glad to get off after their three years." What he did not realize (or did not care about) was that his callous attitude created a growing resentment. Once again, this conflict went unaddressed until it was too late. When the mutiny came, the board led it.

All of these conflicts sat unresolved in the heart of our church, extremely painful things that had been swallowed by the church and in some cases by the pastors and boards. This was the reason why we came on the retreat—God was speaking to our church. He had a message for it. He had been telling the leadership for years about the damage that these unresolved issues continued to cause. Pain was His megaphone. Two discouraged pastors had left and one (me) desperately wanted out because of these unresolved conflicts.

Are you prepared to analyze your church's history and see what it reveals? What repeated patterns might show up? What might God be trying to tell you corporately?

Summary. You need to map your church's "spiritual journey." For this exercise, you need key people and some concentrated time, usually a retreat setting is best. Get an overview of the journey and divide the journey into stages. The pastor should become a student being taught about the church—how it started, how God blessed it in each period, what the challenges were and what conflicts the church faced.

In doing this exercise, the group will begin to see patterns lost in the day-to-day ministry of the church. There may be some resistance when you come to the bad times, a desire to pass over them quickly, "forgetting the things which lie behind." Do not do this. Chances are, this is where you will hear God speak most clearly to your church about what is wrong in its heart.

As important as the blessings, challenges and conflicts have been to understand, there is one final area more crucial than all the others.

Chapter 7

FOCUS ON THE CRISES: GOD'S CORPORATE PASS-FAIL EXAMS

There is a presupposition we must agree on at this point. The presupposition is this: *God has been at work sovereignly leading and teaching your church and the times of His most significant corporate lessons have revolved around crises.* Those crises are the places on the journey *where God tested your church "to see what was in your (corporate) heart"* (Deut. 8:2). Because church leaders seldom think about the corporate heart, these tests often go unrecognized. It is not that the leaders deny there were crises. No one doubts that they were crises; its just that no one realized they were also a God-given revelation of what was in the church's heart.

The nature of the crises. Many churches have faced major crises over contemporary worship styles (you are not alone with this one), over change in the service format, over moving to a new location, over a sudden $100,000 drop in the general fund, over the adultery of one of your key leaders, over a rift in doctrine. Each of these is an example of God's corporate pass-fail exams. They are the church equivalents of the rebellion of Korah (Numbers 16; some group—be it old or young—feels they know better than the leadership on how to lead worship), to the bitter waters of Marah (Exodus 15; a corporate response to disappointed expectations) and the lack of food on the way to Sinai (Exodus 16; a corporate response to privation), or to the sin with the Moabite women (Numbers 25; a corporate response to idolatry, sexual temptation, and failure).

God tests your church to see what is in its heart. He also tests the church leadership as He tested Moses, Aaron, and Miriam. Such parallels should not surprise us. Paul wrote the believers in Corinth about things happening with them that parallel Israel's wilderness wanderings (1 Cor. 10:1-12). In a crisis, leaders get tested in their relationships—to God, to one another, and to the congregation. Depending on your response, Christ has a message for your church—if you pass, there is encouragement and blessing (as with the Ephesians and the false apostles—Rev. 2:2); if you flunk, there is admonition and a challenge to get it right (as with the spiritual leaders in Pergamum who tolerated those who proclaimed error and led people astray—Rev. 2:14-16).

The reality is your church may have faced crises *before you ever got there* and *never learned from them*. Depending on the nature of the crisis, God may not let the church move on and accomplish good, purpose-driven, visionary objectives until these lessons are learned. Attempting to do so will result in frustration or worse, another burnout/dropout to ministry.

Start with the biggest. You are now at the point in the review of your church's history where you have doubtless hit upon some of these crises. Start with the biggest. Don't rush through this discussion; pick each crisis apart and thoroughly understand the dynamics of what took place. Be sure you have as much documentation as possible—church records, board minutes, letters and any other first-hand material to substantiate exactly what transpired.

A biblical illustration may help here. In 2 Samuel 21, Israel experiences a three year famine. David goes to God, seeking to learn from the crises. God tells him the present famine is because of "Saul's bloody house." Saul, during his regime, had violated a covenant Joshua made by seeking to eradicate the Gibeonites. God disciplined the whole community/country because of the actions of a king who lived some twenty-five to thirty years before. *It fell to the present leadership of the country to do what was essential to make things right concerning that past wrong.* God had not let the country/leadership off the hook, despite their ignorance of what had happened or the fact that they were not directly responsible for it. The famine (pain) was God's megaphone to get their attention (which it did). We may protest, "That's not fair!" but it is the way of God. He sees a connected stream from the past community to the present community. Though the perpetrators have passed from the scene, there has been no release of responsibility. The community continues to pay the price until the present leaders do what is necessary to make things right.

There is another passage in the New Testament to illustrate the same principle. Jesus in Matthew 23 pronounces woes upon the scribes and Pharisees for their hypocrisy. One of the charges He lays on them in verses 29-32 regards the past:

Woe to you, teachers of the law and Pharisees, you hypocrites! You build tombs for the prophets and decorate the graves of the right-eous. And you say, 'If we had lived in the days of our forefathers, *we would not have taken part with them in shedding the blood of the prophets.' So you testify against yourselves that you are the descendants of those who murdered the prophets. Fill up, then, the measure of the sin of your forefathers!" (NIV)*

Here we have a new generation that seeks to divorce themselves from the actions of the previous generations. "We are more enlightened now," they are saying. "If we had lived back then, knowing what we know now, we would never have been party to killing the prophets." They let themselves off the hook because that was then and this is now. "Yes, that was a rotten past, but we have grown since then. We have forgotten what lies behind and are reaching forward to what lies ahead!"

Jesus puts them right back on the hook. In admitting that they are organically connected to those who committed the sins for which there was never any repentance and responsibility taken, they bear the guilt *in the present.* Chances are these people Jesus quotes are not actually the direct physical descendants of the perpetrators. It does not matter. Jesus sees an organic connection because they belong to Israel. Do I need to tell you that this principle has *huge* implications to a lot of churches? Things have gone on under previous pastoral regimes and no one has ever taken responsibility for it. The guilt remains and the congregation and spiritual leaders continue to carry it.

These two passages have far reaching implications not only for churches that have had painful crises, but also for any criminal or sinful historic issue in government, a business, a city or a community. I believe God allows the effects of these evil events to continue to have an impact on their arena until those in charge take responsibility for them.

Our crises. Though our church leaders had listed the conflicts (many unresolved) the first major crisis came about sixteen years into the tenure of the first pastor (twenty-two years in the past from the time of our retreat), and it was bloody. The church had voted in a new board of elders. The sitting chairman of the board was the choir director. Many of the board members were hostile to the pastor. The pastor walked into the first board meeting, looked around at the make up of the board and said, "Before we do anything at all, I want a vote of confidence from this board on this pastor's ministry at this point!" He refused to talk about anything else until the board had taken the vote.

While he waited, they voted. Out of the nine men on the board, eyewitnesses told us, seven voted no confidence, one voted in favor of the pastor and one abstained. "So be it!" he said. "I cannot work with this board." With that statement he walked out, leaving the stunned board members behind in the room.

This pastor, who had accomplished so much in planting and leading this church in its growth and evangelistic ministry, styled himself as a "street fighter." Made of the tough entrepreneurial gristle many successful church planters have, he was not going to go quietly into the night. His ownership (versus stewardship) of the ministry was too high and he was ready to fight for it against this power play, no matter what it meant. The board and church found out what that meant the next Sunday. After preaching the morning message, he announced he had a letter to read (which we found in the archives). The essence of the letter is captured in these few sentences.

"I am hereby submitting my resignation to the church . . . I do not believe God is calling me away from the church at this time, but I cannot work with this board. Therefore I am calling a church meeting in two weeks to vote on whether you will accept my resignation."

It does not require long reflection to imagine how this immediately polarized the church. Letters and phone calls began to fly back and forth. One group circulated a petition in favor of the pastor against the board. The next Sunday the chairman of the board fired back with a letter leveling a blast at the petitioners, accusing them of mounting "an American-style political campaign." There may be low insults in Canada, but none lower than that.

The day of the congregational vote came. The association to which the church belonged sent in a mediator. Poor man. The meeting was rancorous, with shouting and threats and things said that, once uttered, were hard to take back or forget. At the end of two hours, they took a vote. The results were fifty-four in favor of the pastor staying, and forty-five against. The pastor was heard to say, "They want me, so I am staying."

He stayed, but the church reeled. The whole board resigned, the majority of Sunday School teachers resigned. The whole choir, except for one woman, quit; all the instrumentalists walked out too. The next week the exodus began. As this story was being related during our retreat, men began to weep openly. I choke up when I remember the pain of these godly people recounting those agonizing days. This occurred twenty-two years before and retelling the events in such detail allowed them to relive the emotions of the experience as if they were yesterday. It also became crystal clear that the wound was still open and unhealed.

"I have never understood how something like this could happen among people who all love God, who all say they believe in Him," said one of the veterans of this split. I have heard it many times from other survivors of such spiritual catastrophes. Another person described that period of the church like being in a war. He did not know who among his friends would be the next casualties and be missing from their pews from Sunday to Sunday. "Coming to church in that period was one of the most painful things I have ever done," he explained. In the span of a month, two hundred and fifty of five hundred people had left, leaving the church with few leaders for its many ministries.

That was just the beginning of hostilities. Two events of this time were of particular note. The first event (described through clenched teeth) was about a large group, almost a hundred members, who began to attend the same church nearby, a small church plant that had about fifty in attendance. This struggling church tripled in size in one Sunday while our church had been gutted!

But that wasn't all. The second event was like salt in the wound. The choir and musicians had stuck together as part of this group. After one Sunday at this church plant, they practiced the next Wednesday and sang as the new church's choir the following Sunday! The loss of the whole music ministry—so visible a part of our church's Sunday worship—was just too much. I believe this loss symbolized the total loss, the lightning rod for much of the grief and anger still carried in the heart of our church.

The two hundred fifty people remaining licked their wounds and tried to recuperate, but the church was sick at heart now. For about six months they struggled with their grief. Finally the new church board (made up of the pastor's followers) met over a weekend without the pastor to try to plan for the future. After much prayer and grieving, they decided that they must ask the pastor to consider leaving. This time he did not fight them. He agreed that his ministry was at an end and resigned.

His departure caused another one hundred and twenty five pastor-loyalists to leave. Twice now board actions had created splits and within a year a church of five hundred was down to about eighty adults. *In the heart of our church a suspicion of board leadership was born—an attitude that had remained for twenty-two years.* This remarkable fact jumped out at the people on the retreat. The congregation's inexplicable resistance and mistrust the board had recently experienced, started with this series of crises. I did not need to emphasize the value of what we were doing any longer—they were convinced! They saw how it directly applied to the pain that they had experienced.

The few families left after the split wondered what would happen to them. They decided to hang in there. In a sense they formed a strong nucleus for a new ministry, since both the fanatically anti-pastor element and the fanatically pro-pastor element were gone. That left the "pro-church element," people who believed that God had called them to the church in that location and they were to stay until God said otherwise.

What is Jesus saying to us? It was time to return to the key question: what was Jesus trying to teach our church through this gut-wrenching series of events?

What our church experienced is, as a country preacher would say, "as common as fleas on a country dog's back." There are so many churches in North America over ten years old that have experienced splits or group exoduses. Their causes may differ—philosophical, doctrinal, personality or power-driven—but these traumas to Christ's body leave scars with varying degrees of seriousness. All of them affect the present ministry of the church if no one ever addressed them. In other words, all of them would have divine messages attached to them; Jesus' directions to His local churches in what they corporately need to do to be able to serve Him effectively again. It is the job of church leadership to discern and address these issues; it is their good work.

Summary. To get immediately to the heart of some of what God is saying to your church, focus on the crises in your church's history. If pain is God's megaphone, He speaks loudest in crises. Start with the biggest crisis first. Tell the stories surrounding it. Allow people the freedom to release their emotions as they recall the painful things. Examine how the events surrounding the crisis have had an ongoing impact in the church. Determine how the church has reacted and/or protected itself from a repeat of the crisis.

Only when the church leadership understands what God was saying by these painful events is it ready to determine how to heal the heart of the church.

Chapter 8

DETERMINE THE RESPONSE OF LEADERSHIP

You, as church leaders, have gone through your history; you have relived its crises. If you, as a pastor, are like most fellow-pastors, you wish you had begun to ask these questions when you first arrived at your church. It would have saved you from so much pain. Now the cathartic exercise is completed. You have begun to put some of the patterns of your church's behavior in context. You have felt the power of the "Aha!!" and the discovery of the origins of attitudes, sensitivities, and values rooted deep in your church's heart. If you have done well, you have connected to your church's history emotionally and spiritually. You are ready to ask the all-important questions: What is God trying to teach us through this? *What is Jesus' corporate message to our church?*

I picture young King Josiah discovering the scroll of Deuteronomy and reading it for the first time. He loved his God and loved his people. He had tried to follow God in his own heart and lead the country to achieve God's purposes. What he failed to understand was the impact of the country's history on his efforts. Upon reading the warnings of Deuteronomy, he tore his clothes, humbled himself, and wept (see 2 Kings 22:19). Josiah understood clearly the reasons Judah was in its present state. He called the leadership of the country together to meet at the temple and decide what to do (see 2 Kings 23:1-6).

Now is your time for the same kind of council before God. Ask the initial question: "What has God shown us that remains unfinished, unresolved from our history? What issues do we need to address to make things right? Where do we see continued effects from these wounds of the church's past?"

Write the letter you believe Jesus would write to your church. This is a powerful way to transition from reflection to action, one in which all who attend the retreat can participate. The model for such a letter is in Figure 4 below. This letter is repeated in the appendix.

The Letter of Jesus to the Eighth Local Church – Ours!

Jesus wrote the seven letters of Revelation 2 and 3 to seven local churches with a variety of issues on His heart. He still speaks to local churches and has messages for them based on His Word. Assess what Jesus might be saying to your church. Write a letter in the format of the letters to the seven churches that you think Jesus might send to your local church.

Salutation: Some characterization of Jesus, attributes which might be apropos to your church.
Example: *"To the angel of the church in Ephesus write: The One who holds the seven stars in His right hand, the One who walks among the seven golden lampstands, says this:'"(Rev. 2:1 NASV)*

Clear Commendation: Jesus usually finds things to commend in the church. What would He commend in your church?
Example: *'I know your deeds and your toil and perseverance, and that you cannot endure evil men, and you put to the test those who call themselves apostles, and they are not, and you found them to be false; and you have perseverance and have endured for My name's sake, and have not grown weary. . . 'Yet this you do have, that you hate the deeds of the Nicolaitans, which I also hate' (Rev. 2:2-3,6).*

Constructive Criticism: Jesus puts His finger on some key issues at present and historically in the church. What would He point out as needing to be addressed in your local church?
Example: *'But I have this against you, that you have left your first love' (Rev. 2:4).*

Crucial Counsel: There is something your church needs to do to get right with Him again.
Example: *'Remember therefore from where you have fallen, and repent and do the deeds you did at first; or else I am coming to you, and will remove your lampstand out of its place—unless you repent.' (Rev. 2:5)*

Promise to the Courageous: Those who do what Jesus says in the advice portion will "overcome" the obstacles to their growth and are promised some amazing things. What would He promise your people if they are courageous to do what He says?
Example: *'He who has an ear, let him hear what the Spirit says to the churches. To him who overcomes, I will grant to eat of the tree of life, which is in the Paradise of God' (Rev. 2:7).*

Figure 4

As a result of this assessment, you will be able to summarize the lessons the leaders have learned from the retreat(s) and begin to craft a leadership response that will lead to healing the heart of your church.

I think the healing can be categorized into three essential steps: steps for the pastor, for the leadership as a whole, and for the church.

The pastor and identificational repentance. Pastors can be the cause of some of the issues, but they may also be victims. Remember Matthew 23 and the fact that though things may have happened under a pastor several pastorates before your coming, you stand in the stream of those who carry the title "pastor." Your enlightenment and acknowledgment that you would never have been party to what the previous pastor did, does not exempt you or excuse you from dealing with the wound that pastor caused to the church.

John Dawson, in his excellent book *Healing America's Wounds* (Regal Books, 1997), describes a concept called "identificational repentance." Identificational repentance flows from an understanding of mediatorial authority. In identificational repentance, I recognize how I identify or am identified with the perpetrator(s) of an injustice or injury. Because I am identified with him/them, I can *stand in their place* and shoulder the responsibility they never did. By so doing, I can enable people to release the pain and anger they may have internalized, extend forgiveness, and, most importantly, experience reconciliation.

God never holds us in bondage to the actions of another. We can always forgive someone (and should) for the injuries they may have caused us and thus find release from the effects of anger and bitterness. However, *forgiveness alone never produces reconciliation with the offender*. Reconciliation requires that *both*–the perpetrator and the victim, the offender and the offended–take steps. It cannot occur until the offender has taken full responsibility for the wrong committed, take ownership of the pain it may have caused, and sought forgiveness. When the offended party extends forgiveness, there can be reconciliation. The two parties can build a relationship.

Given my prior tendency for martyrdom, I had to think this issue through extremely carefully. I had to become biblically convinced that taking responsibility for a prior pastor's problem was within the scope of my spiritual authority. This was not the same as saying, "It's all my fault." As the present pastor of my church, I stand in the stream of all previous pastors and represent them. If there are some who did harm to the church, I can stand in their place and take responsibility before God and the congregation for what they did and seek forgiveness. In a biblical example, in Jesus' day the ones who adorned the monuments of the prophets needed to take responsibility for the sins their fathers committed.

I will not forget the Sunday I did this—and neither will the people who witnessed it. I was preaching on the importance of reconciliation as a prerequisite to answered prayer. God has unusual ways of confirming that we are doing exactly the right thing. The following story became the first in a string of "God-things" that began to occur in our church.

We had two vibrant teenage sisters that had been a part of our youth ministry for years. They regularly prayed for their father to come to Christ and their family to come to church. However, many years had gone by with little or no spiritual interest expressed by their dad. This particular Sunday he woke up with a start, looked at his wife and said, "I've got to go to church today!"

She looked at him through sleepy eyes. "What?" she moaned. "Church? Why on earth do you want to go to church?"

"I don't know," he said. "It's the strangest thing. I just know I *have* to go." So he got up and got dressed. Even his two daughters slept in that Sunday, but he was undeterred. He came and, as he testified later, sat enthralled.

At the end of the sermon I stepped down from of the pulpit and stood in front of the congregation. I took off my suit jacket since few wore suits. Then I said with total honesty, "There's some reconciliation work I need to do now with all of you. The pastors of this church have not always been the shepherds they should have been to you. I have not always been the pastor I should have been for you. I have let some of you down, not been there when you really needed me. *I* have not always been attuned to your heart cries, nor have I been the greatest model of what Christ intended a pastor should be. I have been insensitive and caught up in my own agenda for the church at times. If you've never felt this from me, I daresay there has probably been a pastor in your history that has hurt you or let you down. I also want to stand in his place today, and ask you to forgive me."

Our church was not a "crying" church, nor am I a crier, but many were moved by that moment. I could see tears and hear sniffles, and all across our sanctuary individuals forgave me, some saying it out loud. Their actions served another purpose—forgiving the man or men who had hurt them in the past.

The unsaved dad who had felt such urgency to come to church sat there with his mouth open. He couldn't believe what he had heard. "It was as if God spoke right to me," he said later. "My problem with God had always been the men who represented Him. I had seen pastors and televangelists that were little more than crooks and con men. Now here was a man asking that this barrier be taken out of the way. I not only forgave him, but that same day I opened my heart to God and asked Christ to forgive me for all my sins."

Categories of identificational repentance. A pastor who takes this identificational repentance position can stand for a number of different groups. He can stand for spiritual leadership as a whole, for husbands (if he is married), for fathers (if he has children), for an ethnic group (necessary for racial reconciliation), for males (for the sake of women who have been hurt by them). He can stand for the younger generation to speak to those older; or he can stand for the older generation to speak to those younger. Remember, never do something like this for effect or to manipulate your church. Only do this from a broken, honest heart. Only then will it have the greatest, lasting impact.

Let me give another illustration of how identificational repentance removes historic barriers. As I was learning about mediatorial authority, I attended a weeklong prayer conference run by several pastors in my prayer group. I was extremely anxious about it because the preponderance of people at this conference were from a different doctrinal position and were charismatic in their worship. I knew that if this type of worship were the focus, I would be extremely uncomfortable. The organizers were sensitive, encouraging attendees to respect each other's differences by leaving their normal worship practices out in the parking lot.

The conference had a strong emphasis on the importance of Christians, whatever their differences, agreeing before God in their prayers. When believers break down the walls between them, there is hope that God hears their collective cries for their city and country. The Holy Spirit convicted me about the attitude I brought into the conference toward those of Pentecostal and charismatic persuasion. God would not let me alone about this. I knew I was critical of these brethren because they disagreed with me doctrinally and because I believed their emotionality made them susceptible to error. To be honest, I had made fun of them in the past because I was uncomfortable around them. God was not asking me to change my convictions about doctrine; He was asking me to change my attitude about people for whom He died.

The organizers announced a prayer meeting for pastors the next morning before the conference. The Holy Spirit impressed on me that I should go to that prayer meeting and ask those pastors to forgive me. I tried to convince myself that the feeling was just indigestion and would pass after a good nights' sleep. I woke early the next morning with the same conviction, only stronger. I wrestled with God during my quiet time. I did not want to humiliate myself like this. Please God, no. But God would not let me go. Finally I resigned myself to it and went.

The prayer meeting was horrible, more horrible than I could have imagined. In that prayer meeting of about twenty-five pastors, they played out every stereotype I had of them—long emotional prayers with babbling and convulsing and whooping that seemed so totally senseless to me. All the time God's Spirit kept saying to my heart, "Do it! These are My children. Your attitude is wrong. This is not about them but about *you*! You let Me deal with them. You take responsibility for your attitude!"

I couldn't do it. The words stuck in my throat. I left the prayer meeting and the conference totally defeated. I had faced the "giants and walled cities" of God's very clear will and backed off in fear and loathing at what it meant.

However, God did not let me go. Six months later my church and I were asked to participate in a concert of prayer in our city being held at the largest Pentecostal church in the area. A week before the event, the organizer called and asked me to open the meeting with a short devotional. And God said, "Gotcha! Since you were unwilling to humble yourself before twenty-five you must now do it before 1000!"

So I did. I stood for myself and confessed. But I also went a step further. I acted as the identificational representative of all those of my church and my doctrinal ilk and confessed the attitudes of disrespect and devaluation that kept the body of Christ divided. I spoke briefly on 1 John 4:20: "If someone says, I love God,' and hates his brother, he is a liar; for he who does not love his brother whom he has seen, how can he love God whom he has not seen?" As I finished I was barely in control. With voice cracking, I asked for forgiveness on behalf of myself and my brethren. The other pastors on the platform surrounded me, praying and rejoicing at being able to forgive. They asked my forgiveness for similar attitudes they had. They said they had often taught that those who did not practice the charismatic gifts were second-class kingdom citizens. Needless to say, what followed was an extraordinary prayer meeting.

This is the significance of mediatorial authority. Had I been a lay person, I could have confessed *personal* attitudes, but I could *not* have stood for the church as a whole, nor for pastors. Mediatorial authority allows for identificational repentance.

Church boards and identificational repentance. Second, if there were issues with boards during the church's past history, a similar process of identificational repentance should be done by the current board. Taking responsibility for these issues, it would be appropriate in some context, like around a Lord's Table celebration, for the boards together or the chairperson(s) of the board(s) to stand and similarly ask for forgiveness for the ways the board(s) has/have failed to meet the church's needs. No board is perfect, so this is no lie—not even a small stretch of the truth.

Moreover, the board needs to identify with the previous boards of the church, the ones in the past that may have been responsible for doing significant harm, hurts that no one had confessed or forgiven. The people who were directly hurt by these board actions may be gone and replaced by a new group, but chances are many in this new group have also been hurt in some way by spiritual leadership along the way. The board can stand in the place of those leaders as well and seek forgiveness.

Unfortunately, many churches have been victims of financial impropriety by a previous board member, either by embezzling church funds or lifting some out of the offering before it was deposited. Maybe there was a board "power play" or an attempt to circumvent a church constitution to get something it wanted. If any of these historical scenarios were true for your church, a present board member may say, *"We had nothing to do with those things! We are not responsible for those sins. How can we confess them honestly?"* Remember what we learned from Matthew 23. *Present enlightenment and even present innocence does not release leaders from responsibility for the sins committed by previous generations of spiritual leaders. Those former leaders never took the responsibility for their sin and the sin remains unless we take responsibility for it.* We wear their mantle. The guilt of their sin remains before God and comes out in congregational pain, suspicion and reactivity. Moreover, most board members would admit to being *tempted* during times of congregational stress to opt for less than ethical means to achieve some purpose, even if they did not *act* upon it. Their hearts are no different than those who perpetrated the evil.

We stand in their place now and have a choice. God waits for us to own the sin because we are a part of the stream of leadership that has flowed from that time. The good news is God says we can do something about it and help heal the heart of the church if we have the moral courage. It is a choice though. We can say no. However, the sin (and the congregational pain) remains.

Healing for the church. The third step in healing involves the church. This is especially important if there has been a split, but also if there have been unhealthy corporate situations in the church (pastoral abuse or immorality, gossip, sharp traditional vs. contemporary conflict, prejudice, racism and such). Good leadership addresses the things about which Christ is speaking. How to bring about this healing is the subject of the following chapters.

Here is a word of hope. I undertook this challenge when things were about as low as they could go for me in the ministry to my church. I did not want to be there, I am not sure they wanted me there, and I did not feel I could lead them anymore. I would have measured the hope of any success to be extremely slim at best. I have come to believe that when you address the corporate issues that are on the heart of Christ, you get a *lot* of divine support. Mountains begin to move.

Summary. How should the leadership respond to the painful things discovered in a historical review of your church? The key is in the concept of identificational repentance. Identificational repentance is a unique function of mediatorial authorities, where they can stand in the place of others (because of their position) from the past who may have perpetrated sinful things upon a church. From their position "identifying with the perpetrator," they repent and seek forgiveness from those who have been injured.

This powerful act enables many individuals in the church to release their hurt to Christ. The corporate impact is to heal the heart of the church that has carried the historical wound. There are types of corporate wounds where the process of healing differs, but all of them draw on the power of identifi-cational repentance.

— LEADING THE CONGREGATION TO HEALING —

Chapter 9

LEADING THE CONGREGATION TO HEALING: SPLITS

The good work of leadership has one final step in the process to complete the healing in many churches. That step may be different based on the kind of crises that wounded your church. The following chapters outline various kinds of corporate church wounds and approaches to their healing.

Let's review. You have surveyed the church's spiritual journey and uncovered the historical roots of its problems. As church leadership, you have identified the things Christ has been saying to your church through its pain. You have taken pastoral and leadership steps to address your parts in the reconciliation process through identificational repentance. You have also strengthened your leadership position as the mediatorial authorities in your church by these actions. If necessary, you are now ready to lead the church—the corporate body—to do its part in healing.

There are a small number of churches that would not need this step. They are rare. It may be that the historic sin truly has been on the part of leadership alone. In many cases though the congregation has participated in the sin or reacted badly to the sin of others and needs its own healing. Extending forgiveness is one side of this, but they may also need to seek forgiveness themselves. This is especially true in the case of a split or where a pastor has been made a victim or congregational scapegoat, either once or as a pattern.

I believe you will have Christ's full and evident assistance at this point. You will see Him facilitating the deeper corporate healing that needs to take place because the mediatorial leadership has humbled itself and obeyed Him. You will need His unmistakable assistance because not everyone in the congregation will understand what you are doing no matter how much you explain it. Some that do understand what you are doing will still think you are either unbalanced mentally or flat-out wrong. You should anticipate resistance from some key individuals, especially those who have vested interests in the status quo (a controlling person or family, a key giver, the "loyal opposition" who resist everything you try to do, or some who will react to all this "touchy-feely" stuff). Christ's assistance does *not* mean everyone will be happily on board, so do not let the naysayers discourage you at this point. Your elected leadership should be with you and that is enough. Mediatorial authority carries the ability to pull this off.

We need to examine the various strategies to approach the necessary repentance, cleansing and restoration of the heart of the congregation in the case of a split, in the case of pastor abuse, in the case of sinful reactivity, and in the case of past corporate shame.

Dealing with a Split. I remember reading an article about the history of the Church in the Canadian prairies, a section of which was entitled "The Bifurcated Baptists." My vocabulary being weak, I went running to my dictionary to find out if this were a new denomination of Baptist that I had never heard of before and started to laugh when I saw the definition. Bifurcated means "split."

Unfortunately (or, if you are a Baptist, fortunately I guess) the Baptists do not have a corner on the market when it comes to church splits. Splits have occurred in the churches of every denomination and association; few independent churches escape them either. They occur for just about every reason you can name, from the choice of carpet color, to the Bible translation being used, to the music choice, to doctrinal heresy. Any reason a church splits is embarrassing to the testimony of Christ. There are no noble splits. Something has gone so wrong in the Body of Christ that amputation is the only perceived solution. People who once shared a common vision and worked side by side can no longer communicate civilly. People who had been close friends for years find themselves on opposite sides of horrific conflicts that tear the fabric of their friendship apart. Now they no longer speak. This spiritual violence done to the Body of Christ has become commonplace. Like serial divorces, one split sets the stage for more. If a church has avoided working out its conflicts through splitting, splitting then becomes a "normal" way to handle conflicts. People leave rather than work out their problems.

Splits leave long-term and ongoing damage to the heart of a church. The week that I write this I've had a discussion about splits with two couples from a church where I was invited to speak. "Our church split nine years ago," one of the women said. "We are still feeling the effects of it." She paused, then sighed, and said with deep sadness, "I don't think churches *ever* heal from splits." I assured her they could, but that most church leadership does not know how to go about healing such wounds in the church's heart.

Our church had endured a gut-wrenching split wrapped up in power politics between pastor and Board and an inappropriate sense of "ownership" of the ministry. The church divided itself into warring factions. The winners stayed and the losers left. The trauma of that split froze our congregation in an identity crisis. Remember the statement I heard as I came to candidate, "This church does not know what it wants to be when it grows up." It was thirty-plus years old! It was grown up. However, the trauma that occurred at age seventeen in its history prevented the church from accepting guidance that might have helped it get beyond that adolescent state. It had grieved the loss, but knew no way to resolve the grief. Instead the grief and anger simply went underground into free-floating discontent, inappropriate suspicion, and an unspoken dread of conflict. In that last sense I, as a conflict absorber, was the "perfect pastor" for them. Our dysfunctions were a match.

How do you resolve a split, especially an ancient one? (Actually a recent one is sometimes more difficult because hostile feelings are still fresh and apt to erupt). There are several steps you need to follow.

Mediatorial leaders must lead. First, those with mediatorial authority must lead the church through this process. The congregations of the split groups will be carrying far too much baggage to work through the issues by themselves. The leaders will have their baggage too, but hopefully they will rely on spiritual maturity and obedience to Christ to overcome the obstacles. The leaders of the estranged churches need to find a way to meet and talk about reconciliation.

Understand reconciliation. Reconciliation in this context does not mean reunification. Although there will be some who push for this, unless the split is of extremely recent origins or you can give compelling reasons for such reunification (two struggling churches become one viable church), such efforts are probably doomed to fail. I have rarely heard of two churches, even those that got along famously, who were able to pull off a unification of ministries. Once differentiation has taken place in church ministry, a new leadership and a new pastor established, a new constitution drawn up or embraced, there is little hope of reunification.

Reconciliation *does* mean the cleansing of the corporate conscience and resolving the anger and grief that lay in the corporate hearts of the two bodies. That unclean conscience and corporate wound create many of the sinful symptomatic evidences of reactivity about which Jesus has been speaking to your church. You cannot progress until these are resolved.

God never binds us to an unclean conscience if the party with whom we seek to reconcile is unwilling to do so. We can still make amends or humble ourselves to ask forgiveness, which is proper and biblical to do, whether they forgive or not. God cleanses us and allows us to be free, even if the estranged people will not. It is *not possible* to get such cleansing by ignoring the party estranged from us because we do not want to face them. We *will* have to talk with them.

Contact the other pastor(s). Where and how do we begin? Pastors are the key figures here, the ones Ted Haggard, author of *Primary Purpose* (Creation House, 1995), calls "the gatekeepers of the city." Pastors of the estranged congregations need to make contact, however awkward and difficult it may be. They may need to meet on neutral turf and do whatever may be necessary to allow them the chance to communicate for the good of their churches.

What do they talk about? They should address some of the unhealthy things that are occurring in their congregations that have their roots in the split and, once they are identified, the focus should turn to the need for reconciliation to be right with God. If one of the pastors has worked through the steps presented in this book, *he should take the initiative and explain the things that Christ has been saying to his church*. He should not force the other pastor to do anything and should definitely not blame him or the other congregation for anything. Even a hint of blame will shut down communication immediately. Explaining the things Christ has been addressing in his own congregation will help make the need to take some sort of action very evident.

Consider all the options. The kinds of actions open to the congregations are many and varied. As a counselor, one of the most common defenses I heard against a recommended action to speed healing in individuals or families was for them to believe there were limited options. Usually the options were limited to two alternatives—my current position and some ridiculous alternative. The latter sounds like: "If we come and humble ourselves and seek forgiveness from them, that sends the message they did not do anything wrong, that it is all our fault. We won't do that!" Of course *that* action does *not* preclude *that* result, but the assumption that it does maintains the status quo.

You have to get past the "limited options" thinking and explore the vast array of possibilities. The two pastors should brainstorm and come up with a list of the possibilities about which they can pray, or find one that resonates as right and appropriate.

What are some of those options? Although such a reconciliation service does not require reunification, maybe you are in one of those rare situations where everyone has regretted the split. If so, you can have a full-blown reconciliation service where, at the end, the two divided churches unite again. Other churches have had services on their own, sending out invitations or calling former members and pastors, inviting them back for reconciliation. Many sensitive people will respond to such an invitation for they will feel in their souls the damage the split has done. I had one young man tell me about his grandmother who left our church in the split. "She was never the same spiritually after that," he said. "She had been so active, but after the split she never volunteered for anything in the church ever again." Splits create that kind of pain in the hearts of people. Such a person could have turned that around with a meaningful reconciliation.

Determine the where and when. You should make some attempt to reach and invite the estranged members to such a service. Fortunately, I had come to know the pastor of the church where the choir had gone after our split. Twenty-two years had passed and that church was now a well-established, thriving ministry. We had become prayer partners and slowly built a deep, trusting friendship before I began to deal with these issues in my church. He had been at his church a little longer than I had been at mine, but he was mostly unaware of the split. His church had undergone something just short of a split before he came (he called it a "minor exodus.") Later I learned that a number of the people behind our church's split had an active part in his church's "exodus." This didn't surprise me.

As he and I discussed the situation, the idea of a reconciliation service came up. I was enthusiastic but he was not certain about it. He felt that the majority of the people in his church would not know why they were doing this—essentially reconciling with events that had occurred twenty-two years earlier. His church had grown quite large and there were only a handful of people left from those days. The pastor agreed that something needed to be done, but could the issues be laid to rest without emphasizing the ancient split?

At first I was disappointed with his response as I had envisioned a full joint reconciliation service, both parties confessing sin and asking forgiveness of the other. Not mentioning the split seemed to defeat the whole purpose of the exercise. However, I remembered that God never ties His ability to heal us to the actions of another. We did not need his church to do *anything* for us to deal with our wounds. Moreover, I respected his wisdom and his choice as the mediatorial authority of that congregation.

Finally, we agreed upon a joint Good Friday service held at his church. My congregation would approach it as a reconciliation service, and he graciously facilitated it by making certain we had the freedom to do what we

needed to do. We designed a service filled with symbols for our congregation, but that would minister to all. It began with Good Friday.

Make use of symbols. Symbols are extremely important in reconciliation events, much as they are in covenant making or peace treaties. God
loads His covenants with symbols and signs, from the rainbow to circumci-
sion to bread and a cup. What better time to address the sins and wounds
in the corporate heart of a church than Good Friday? This is what Jesus died
to do (see Eph. 5:23-25).

Now it was up to me, with the support of the boards, to prepare the
congregation for this event five months away. We were in our fortieth year
now, and I had begun to prepare the congregation for that watershed
anniversary, the "generation marker" of Scripture. I had begun to preach
selected passages in Deuteronomy. Deuteronomy provided a great model.
Moses was in the fortieth year of wilderness wanderings, poised on the edge
of a new chapter of history for the people of God. He seized the opportunity to review their spiritual journey as a people and to remember the lessons
God had taught them. (You do not have to be in your fortieth year to review
your church's corporate spiritual journey. The fact of the journey is the key.)

Everyone can identify with life as a journey or quest. The quest is one
of the great dramatic engines driving all human life and much literature.
Whether it is *The Odyssey* or *The Hobbit*, life as a journey and quest captures
the imaginations of people. There is tension and drama throughout such a
quest. Will Odysseus succumb to the Siren's song? Will the Golem catch and
kill Frodo? When people realize they have joined a church on such a quest,
it isn't negative. Quite the contrary.

Moses wanted to rehearse the history of the journey for the many new
people that were now a part of the congregation of Israel. The old-timers
were mostly gone, but the history of those early days mattered to everyone—
who they were and *why* they were *where* they were. Many of these lessons
were not positive; some were downright painful. I have seen churches that
publish such a history as a part of significant church anniversaries. Invariably
though these histories are sanitized. They only tell the positive. Moses pulled
no punches in reminding the children of Israel the hard lessons of the wilderness, of the rebellions and disobedience and unbelief. I would not pull
punches either.

Plant the seeds of future vision. Often pastors, especially pastors
who take over pre-existing churches, fail to connect their vision of the future
with the church's spiritual journey and where they are right now. One can
see the importance of doing this because it helps prepare for the formation
of a vision to come. Remember that you are doing these things to prepare

the congregation for those important tasks of developing a vision for the future and purpose-driven objectives. They miss the lessons God has been trying to teach the church, lessons they may not yet have learned. The very things that will prevent a vision from being successful, will derail a vision before it gets too far. Planting seeds at this point helps prepare the congregation for the important tasks of developing a vision for the future and establishing purpose-driven objectives

In our church, during a four month series titled "Celebrate what God has done; Contemplate what God can do," I showed how our church's spiritual journey intersected with Israel's. You don't have to read far in Deuteronomy before Moses reveals what derailed Israel from achieving God's purposes (like chapter 1). I raised the question "Would there be things historically in our spiritual journey as a church this last forty years that Moses would be telling us about? We will find out in the weeks ahead."

Be aware of your audiences as you tell the story. Report such history with three audiences in mind. The first audience is the *new people* who have joined your congregation after some of the crises occurred. They will be curious. They will connect the stories to their own journey and previous church experiences. Hearing the lessons God has taught the church through the painful times could enlighten the newcomers.

The second audience is more problematic—*those who lived through those bad times*. They cannot listen dispassionately. They are going to require that the history be reported accurately. This makes your job more of a challenge if you have done a cursory job of understanding it. If these members were at all involved, you should get their perspective on the material you share. Ask some of the old timers to help review the material you are going to report, especially if the material is sensitive. Most will be eager to give you their perspective.

In addition, if you are going to report something unflattering about a previous pastor, make sure you balance it with the positive things God accomplished through him. God's clear command to mediatorial authorities is to operate "without partiality." Many of the old-timers will have strong opinions, both positively and negatively. A former pastor may have conducted the wedding of a member's daughter or delivered a moving message at a husband's funeral. Prejudiced, unbalanced opinions about a previous pastor on the part of the current pastor could cause all he is working toward to be rejected or worse—unblessed by God. The possibility of prejudice increases if the pastor has experienced serious pain because of the church's reactions to problems caused by a previous minister.

Though our church's founding pastor made a grievous error that split our church, he also was a marvelous evangelist and built the church up through evangelism. He trained numerous pastors and lay people in evangelism. Many of the old-timers came to Christ through his ministry. Moreover, he was not alone in precipitating the crisis. The board that voted "no confidence" played a significant part. There was a process of insensitivity that led up to the crisis also. An honest telling of the history required that I explain all of it.

There is a third audience—your church visitors—you need to keep in mind. They may have no idea why you would be sharing these things. Some of the congregation will be very sensitive to visitors and the things they hear. You should parallel congregational lessons with family lessons. All congregational problems are family problems: whether it is how conflict gets resolved (or not), sin covered inappropriately, rebellion against authority, or corrupted values. If the pastor is sensitive in how he presents the material, visitors may hear their own stories in the church's history, and they may also learn what God may be saying to them through such problems.

Expect to see God confirm your direction. I felt my leadership motivation—so long an issue after the failure of our Matrix vision—rekindled. I *knew* we were doing the right thing! That in itself was extraordinary. Then God confirmed it by doing extraordinary things. They were, however, only the first raindrops of a cloudburst of blessing to come.

One of these extraordinary events was the restart of that previous brood of vipers—the choir. The very woman who had tried to lead the choir thirteen years previously (when she sought to audition the members) led it! God had taught her many things from the church's history, and, with extraordinary courage, she sought to undo personally what had been done thirteen years before. With spiritual sensitivity and faith she reentered that viper's den. I was more than a little afraid that a sour attitude on the choir's part could ruin everything. But things were changing in the heart of our church. This second time she did a marvelous job and the spirit in the choir grew more and more positive. This new choir would ultimately become a key part of the reconciliation process.

Everything and everyone was geared up for that Good Friday service. The plans for the service began to solidify. I had arranged with the other pastor that our choir would minister and one of our instrumentalists would play. We were actually establishing symbols here. We were directly addressing the wound created in and around the music ministry.

Prepare everyone for the event. The story of the split actually fit well into my Palm Sunday sermon. On the first Palm Sunday the hopes of the disciples were sky-high. These hopes were soon shattered by the experiences that occurred afterwards. The disciples' experience paralleled the high hopes many had for our church before the split twenty-two years before. When the split came, those members remaining must have wondered if any good could come from such negative circumstances. For twenty-two years our church had lived in the shadow of those shattered hopes. We had not fully embraced the message God had for us through that painful experience. That was about to change.

I explained exactly what we would do at this neighboring church and why we were doing it. I invited everyone who had a painful experience in a previous church to use the opportunity afforded on Good Friday to ask Christ to forgive whatever sins were involved and heal the wounds. I explained exactly why our choir would sing. The choir would sing in that church as a declaration that God had restored what our church had lost.

We were not trying to be like little children, sticking out our tongues and rubbing it in, "Look what we did! You didn't hurt us!" Rather it would be singing of Christ's forgiveness and blessing God for the restoration He had made. We were able to include another wonderful symbol: our instrumentalist was the son of the one choir member that stayed in our church; the instrumentalist provided by the host church was a musician who had left our church twenty-two years before. Again, most of the members of the host church would not know any of this, but everyone from our church knew the significance of this pairing.

The host pastor permitted me to preach the devotional. I prepared a message from 1 Peter 2:24 called "Healed by His Wounds." My pastoral colleague and host would lead the celebration of the Lord's table, bringing the two churches together in communion. We prayed together that this would do the work of healing we sought for the heart of our church.

Do what is in your heart. Good Friday came and the church was jammed. People were literally sitting on the floor under the coat racks! I'd never seen anything like it. The presence of God was tangible. Mediatorial authorities cannot *make* anything happen of a spiritual nature in people's hearts, but as they operate fully under the Lordship of Christ, they can do all that is in their hearts. Christ Jesus can then work freely. We sensed Him working on that holy day. I called on people to bring not just their sins to Jesus but their wounds. He died not just to forgive sins, but to heal the wounds sin causes. Together we were committed to return to the "Shepherd and Guardian of our souls." The choir sang, the instrumentalists played—all beautifully—and we all shared the communion together.

As I drove out of the parking lot, I got my first hint that something remarkable had taken place in the service. A couple in their 70s, charter members of our church and survivors of the split, were walking to their car holding hands. They saw me and waved me down. "Pastor," the wife said in a voice filled with awe, "that was wonderful. I want you to know that we talked to some people today we have not spoken to in twenty-some years."

That was just the beginning. On Easter Sunday we had a baptism as a part of the service (an Easter tradition for us) and the people being baptized gave testimonies. This is normally an exciting service, but there was an extraordinary air of excitement and joy that day. It was hard for me to know whether I (and everyone else) was still on a "high" from Good Friday. However, we planned the weeks following as "normal church." They were far from normal. Something had changed atmospherically in the church. You could sense it the moment you walked into the building. One guest speaker, who came in the weeks following Good Friday, offered an unsolicited comment to me before the service, "I have never been in a church that had such a thick atmosphere of joy. Is your church always like this?"

Confirmation comes in the increase of "God-things." If one does what God wants, one can rightly expect to see God confirm it. The "God-things" we saw in the buildup to the reconciliation now came in a downpour. For over a year we spent the first hour of our weekly staff meetings just reporting the things each of us was seeing. My favorite story of this period was about the woman who had made loud comments with her husband during my preaching. She was hospitalized with suspected colon cancer. I went to visit her the night before her surgery. With her husband sitting by her bed, she grabbed my hand and said, "Pastor, I have said and thought some terrible things about you. I have carried a horrible attitude toward you. Can you possibly forgive me?"

The honesty and fervency of her confession moved me. "Yes," I said. "No problem. I do forgive you, and I can not tell you how much it means to me." She had her surgery the next day and the polyps suspected to be cancerous were benign. I went to visit her again as she recovered. As I approached her bed, she grabbed my hand again. "Pastor," she said, "I do not want you to think it was just because I faced serious surgery that I wanted your forgiveness. I want you to forgive me on this side of the surgery as well." My favorite part of this was the Wednesday night prayer meeting a couple of weeks later. She did not know I had entered the room at the back. She raised her hand to share a praise item: "I want to praise the Lord for the pastor's messages the last couple of weeks. Is it my imagination or has his preaching really improved?"

For lack of a better description, our church experienced a spiritual renewal. Lives were changing on a weekly basis though we did nothing different than we had done before. People who had been stuck in unhealthy or destructive patterns for years began to change and grow.

Can I guarantee that if you take similar steps you will see similar things? You know I can't do that. It isn't magic or even pragmatic, "Do this and it will work." I believe with all my heart that if you are running into obstacles in your attempts to implement a vision or a strategy for your church, and if the mediatorial leaders in a congregation take seriously the task of finding out what God has been teaching the church through its history, then God will work as you respond to His lessons. Obedience is blessed. It should not surprise us. The Spirit will finally free you. Your church's heart will be healed.

Summary. Arranging for healing a congregation that has had a split in its history begins with the mediatorial leaders (the pastor and the board) taking point and leading. They should fully grasp the principles and limits of doing reconciliation. The pastor of the church seeking healing should contact the pastor of the split congregation and, if that pastor is willing, arrange a joint service filled with symbols.

The pastor seeking healing should prepare his congregation for that service by reviewing the church's journey. If this is done well, though mediatorial leaders can not make anything happen, the Spirit of Christ can work powerfully to set the church free from its bondage and heal its heart. The result will be an outpouring of "God-things" to confirm that the church has left the "paths of pain" and found the eternal path.

Chapter 10

LEADING THE CONGREGATION TO HEALING: PASTORS WHO ABUSE

Many churches today have in their history one of two traumatic experiences. They have either had a pastor who has subjected them to spiritual abuse or they themselves have abused their pastor. Either situation requires work on the corporate heart to produce healing. Either situation (and they may actually be interwoven—a church that has had an abusive pastor can become abusive to the pastors that follow) produces the kind of wound in the corporate heart and impact on the atmosphere to which you know Christ is going to speak. It is going to be hard for a church to move on in its journey if it has not addressed such corporate wounds. Pastoral leadership is at the heart of this wound.

Pastors who abuse. This situation has been lifted into the light in recent years. A plethora of books have been written to describe the dynamics (and the frequency) of spiritual abuse by pastors in a church. This abuse takes a variety of forms—from the control-freak (like Diotrophes in 3 John 9,10) who won't permit any meeting of which he (or his wife) is not a part, to the pastor who seeks to manipulate people to enrich his personal empire (like Simon Magus in Acts 8:18-21). A pastor who abuses can demand an ungodly level of loyalty from his staff that overlooks his indiscretions when he is either immoral or unethical. Some pastors have developed the concept of the "armor bearers"—staff who are required to follow the pastor around and serve him, be aware of his sins but keep their mouths shut. Any criticism or question of the pastor's decisions or behavior is disloyalty, "touching the Lord's anointed." Loyalty like this is what Bertrand Russell referred to when he said, "All loyalty is evil!" We are used to seeing loyalty as a positive trait, but it is not so with a pastor who abuses.

A pastor who abuses, following the lead of despots and dictators through the centuries, creates an outside threat to bind his people to him. He will create a climate of suspicion, fear and danger towards someone or some group: towards all "outsiders," towards all who use a different Bible translation, towards all who counsel or receive counseling, towards anyone who goes to a doctor, towards anyone who questions what he says. They teach and model paranoia about anyone who does not home-school their children, who does not get on the anti-abortion bandwagon, who does not belong to their denomination.

They level regular blasts at prominent Christian leaders, especially those who have been successful in ministry or evangelism, finding fault with something/everything, always creating suspicion about anything that smacks of a connection to these ministries. They create fear of the infiltration of "worldly ideas" into their church. The presence of even one of these ideas is guaranteed to bring on the apostasy before the Apocalypse—whether rainbows because of their New Age connection, psychotherapy because of its secular/worldly methods and promise of healing apart from Christ and the Scriptures, seeker services because they water down/corrupt the Gospel, contemporary Christian music because it is nothing more than an accommodation to the rock-and-roll age, etc. These are all lumped together to intensify an atmosphere of danger and fear.

Am I saying that all the things such pastors are suspicious about are good? That is just the point. *You cannot paint all these issues with one brush—either the "good" brush or the "evil" brush.* Yet some pastors communicate such suspicion and fear creating trauma and paranoia on the part of weak people in their congregations. They are often obsessed with these issues. Thinking people will feel the obsession and oppression and find another church.

It's unlikely you are a pastor like this but what if one of these "pastor despots" preceded you in your present church? Or what if one started the church you've just taken? Would such a ministry create a wound in the heart of the church? I don't need to answer that. The *kind of effects* you would see if this actually was the case in your church is the more significant truth to discover.

CHARACTERISTICS OF AN ABUSED CHURCH

Dependent people. Every church ministry has dependent, vulnerable people in it. These people have had backgrounds of dependency, due to abusive, controlling or absent parents, or chemical dependencies. One of the effects of abusive pastors though is to create and/or attract such dependent people. Sometimes people from such ministries have transferred to my church, and they come in with an unnatural dependency on me for 1) their decision making; 2) what is true; 3) help with their marriage or children; and/or 4) support for their causes. If I didn't provide these services, they got very unsettled, becoming hurt, angry, accusatory, and gossipy. They gravitate toward other weak people to form cliques, usually with a "minor despot" (someone who has problems with your ministry) leading it. Then they feed each other a toxic stew.

A pastor who takes a church where a former pastor abused the people will find large numbers of such dependent people, even if they have risen up to throw the abuser out. That does not necessarily make them ready to receive a new pastor. With good reason some parishioners will be suspicious towards all spiritual authority. Some will just be hurting, filled with a sense of guilt and shame that sensitive preaching and lots of love can cure. Even if several pastors have come and gone since the abusive pastor (unless he came and left very quickly), there will be work to do to build up people.

Weak lay leaders. One of the most distressing aspects of abusive pastors is how they hamstring leadership in a church. Abusive pastors cannot tolerate dissent, so all spiritual leaders who think for themselves and who can speak the truth in love have left for ministries that allow them that freedom. The ones left learn not to talk about anything controversial, showing genuine fear if the conversation gravitates to deeper issues. They may desire to be close and "supportive" of the new pastor, but they will expect a reward for such loyalty.

A pastor who abuses steals the spine out of the other leaders around the church. He chooses people for leadership who don't have much of a backbone to start. He seeks loyalty and "yes-people." Part of the work a new pastor has is to begin to reward those who express their own opinions, to encourage dissent with his opinions and recommendations, to honor those who tell him the truth. "Are you crazy?" you may think. "I am to encourage dissent? I *dream* of a church where no one disagrees with me." That is the subtle temptation that sometimes leads to abuse. An abusive pastor will demonize anyone who dissents or questions what he does. He can make them feel like Satan incarnate.

Such spiritual brutality silences true leaders or they leave. Moving such a brutalized group through the church's history can encourage them to see the effects of the former pastor upon leadership in the church. It is with the leaders that you need also to begin identificational repentance as pastor. They need to hear from you a confession of the evil of a pastor suppressing their voice as mediatorial leaders in the church.

Repressed atmosphere. Abusive pastors are rigid and create a repressed, rigid atmosphere in the church. The shut-down of free expression carries over to the atmosphere, definitely affecting the heart of the church. People repress conflict and joy also. What you see instead, for lack of a better term, is a "fake joy." People will talk about God's blessing. In fact, that is all they will talk about. They seldom will be open about weakness or pain. They considered it "unspiritual" to do so under that previous administration. If someone shares a problem he/she has had, it is always in the past and he/she always has "victory" now. The problem has disappeared, but you never hear about it when they are actually struggling with the problem.

Invariably, this repressed atmosphere creates a buildup of toxic feelings beneath the surface. There is often a lot of "lightning rod discharge" in a church like this. The former pastor focused this energy upon the groups or issues around which he had created fear and suspicion. With those lightning rods gone, the new pastor is apt to have his whole ministry become the lightning rod, especially if people view him as showing sympathy to any of the issues the former pastor opposed. He becomes the focus of the suspicion and can end up the victim of abuse himself. This usually starts to happen fairly quickly, within six months of the start of his ministry. The toxicity builds rapidly after that, and it all depends on the pastor's response and his emotional state as to how long he can hold the lightning rod.

THE CHALLENGES OF AN ABUSED CHURCH

All these symptoms are grievous to a pastor with an open heart and a genuine desire to serve God's people. He can find it extremely frustrating. There are some ways to address these issues as you seek to heal the heart of your church, however, *just as with individuals who have been abused, abused churches are the most challenging of situations to heal.* Just like abused individuals, these churches are also apt to become abusive.

Needless to say, such churches require enormous patience, lots of love, and a fair amount of skill, just like their human counterparts. Most of us come ready to love our people, but we hope they will be somewhat lovable. In the case of abused churches, the free-floating anger toward the leaders who seek to set them free makes them a challenge to love. Like Moses with the congregation of ex-slaves, it took them almost a generation to rid themselves of their rebelliousness toward authority. Like Moses, many a frustrated pastor has taken such rebelliousness personally.

I wish I could offer you more hope, but in reality even doing the church's spiritual journey and identificational repentance may be viewed as highly suspicious. Seeking to find out what Jesus is saying to your church will be placed in a context of doing something dangerous, especially if you wait past the six-month "honeymoon" to do it. Your chances of making progress increase if you do such analysis immediately upon arrival at a church. The only problem is that you may not know you *have* a problem until the six months are up. By then it may be too late. I truly grieve for you. Your task may be to convince the next pastor to do the church's spiritual journey first thing.

Handling the history. Let's assume the best-case scenario. You were concerned by some of the things people reported to you about the previous pastor when you candidated. You want to corroborate their stories. The former pastor actually had a file on every person in the church? He recorded every phone conversation he had with parishioners and kept the tapes? Either he or his wife had to be present at every committee meeting or Bible study? He didn't allow any small groups because he saw them as "gossip covens?" His six children, ages ten and under, didn't move a muscle in the front row during every long service? You talked to this pastor to get his read on the church before you came, and he had nothing kind to say about anyone, warning you about several who were "quite rebellious and influenced by feminist thinking." Hmmmmm. You begin to sense something is not quite right with this picture.

So, feeling God's leading (you are neither blind nor foolish for doing this), you accept the call to this church. As a matter of course, you quickly schedule to take the boards away for a leadership retreat where they will "educate you" in the history of the church. You do this before you take any other initiatives so that you can have some sense of what the church has gone through and where it is. You prime them with some of the things you want to know. You gather together some key "long-timers" to bring along and find out who is the church historian. Have him/her bring some of the pictures that might aid in the storytelling.

You follow the same process as in chapters 6 though 8. It may take three retreats to come to the most recent crises. You may learn how the church has had a pattern of abusive pastors followed by pastors who quickly burn out trying to deal with the dysfunction. You may get the feeling you are looking into a mirror at your potential future. "What is God saying to us through this?" becomes so critical to discern.

HEALING THE HEART OF YOUR CHURCH

Identificational repentance with the leaders. When you have worked through some of the crises precipitated by the abusive pastor (and probably watched a tremendous release of anger and/or grief), your church lay leaders will be strung out and very vulnerable. What you want to do at this point is use your power of identificational repentance as a mediatorial authority. It is time to say something along the lines of *"Look, I have not been a perfect pastor for my congregation(s) in the past. I have certainly felt the temptation to manipulate and control people for the sake of my own agenda or to protect myself from pain. So I want to stand here before you in the place of that former pastor right now and as a pastor ask your forgiveness for the hurt and pain you have endured. He may not know he has done anything wrong and may never acknowledge responsibility for hurting you so badly, but I know. God requires me to take that responsibility as your present pastor according to Matthew 23:29-32. Can you forgive me in his place so that we can move on from here?"*

Done with sensitivity and an honest, sincere heart, this repentance will have a powerful impact on the leaders gathered. Some that may have felt stifled and dependent may finally feel safe to emerge as the leaders God has prepared them to be. The best case scenario will be that it will bind your hearts together with them at the outset of your ministry and increase your chance of success. You will need to follow their turnaround with some exercises and meetings focused upon strengthening them as leaders. Certainly one of the things you need to communicate is *the importance of their mediatorial authority*, for they will have some work to do with this.

Although most leaders will rejoice, some may be uncomfortable with the change in roles from dependent to responsible. You may see resistance that is quite pronounced. Some may simply not trust you as they have learned not to trust pastors. Part of the dysfunction a spiritual abuser creates is a pattern of rigid thinking and beliefs. This rigidity becomes manifest in polarized "good-evil" thinking on the part of his followers, some of whom may still be among the leadership. If something is not in their belief system as "good," it may be demonized. Both in terms of what they perceive to be the "good kind of pastoral authority" (this mean absolute authority, "the Lord's anointed") and any other kind (which is considered evil), they will react with hostility. The ones who react this way may even leave the church or worse, stay and organize opposition. How I could wish I could guarantee it would not happen.

Identificational repentance before the church. If the majority of the church leaders have now responded to your repentance, think together as a group about how you will communicate what you have learned to the entire church. You *must address* the church as a whole, for it is the corporate heart that requires the healing as well as the individuals. The lay leadership in particular needs to play a part in this repentance. Over time, they have not done their part in protecting the flock the way they should. Even if it is a new board with new members, they need to do identificational repentance on behalf of the boards that never did take responsibility for failing to protect the church from the abuse.

You should choose a time and plan a service where again you may establish some symbols of the actions and new direction that are being taken. If you can accomplish this in the first six months, you increase your chances at ministry success. If you suspect you are dealing with an abusive situation, you may want to delay your installation service, common to many churches, and utilize that event to declare these things. If not, name the service something meaningful like "Reconciliation Sunday" or a "Solemn Assembly." Build up to it by preaching a series on "Forgiveness," on "Biblical Leadership," on "Healing Relational Wounds God's Way," or something similar. Don't be afraid to load "Reconciliation Sunday" with significance for the future of the church. Let people know the leadership has something very important to say to them that day that they all need to hear. You want people to feel the importance of the day.

Take your time and do it right. If you are anything like me, the hope that this could turn things around made me want to rush into action before I was ready. Be assured that God is already at work to prepare everyone, that He is much more interested in His church healing than you may be. God-things should be confirming you are on the right track. Be sensitive to the Spirit and follow His lead.

Besides the present congregation, you should also invite those who may have left because of the former pastor's abuse (someone will know about these people or they will be on the church roll). A letter to these former attendees explaining that you are having a reconciliation service will attract them. Communicate that you know there were many that were injured by what took place under the previous administration, and Christ has spoken to the leadership about the need to get this right with those who were hurt. Some of the most devastated people may have sworn never to enter your church again, but under the grace of God they need to break that vow.

Should you invite the former pastor? There would be some rare, happy circumstances that would clearly indicate such an invitation is appropriate. Sometimes these pastors are fresh out of a school or an internship that presented the model of the dictatorial pastor. They are open enough to realize the model didn't work and was as hurtful to them as it was to others. If you have built a relationship with this man and have heard from him that he has learned from what happened, then such an invitation may produce the kind of mutual healing to Christ's Body that one only dreams about. He should be well coached as to what this service is about, and you must have total confidence he won't say or do something destructive. He should be put at the end of the service where he has had a chance to watch repentance in action. Unless your confidence is rock solid though, he presents a large risk. He might also make many people anxious by his presence.

The possibility of reconciliation with him increases *after* the church has gone through reconciliation with you identificationally. They won't be nearly as anxious about his presence. Take this into account as you measure the risk-benefits. Having him back a year after the service when feelings have calmed down and the congregation has more perspective (and trust in your leadership) may make more sense. Some who followed or appreciated him will want this kind of closure and those badly hurt by him will need it. Having a public apology to him at that time for the hurtful things said and/or done to him (in reaction to his treatment—but nevertheless wrong and therefore needing appropriate confession) could go a long way to total healing for the heart of the church. Nevertheless, if he remains unrepentant or unwilling to participate, God never limits our ability to heal by the response (or lack thereof) of the perpetrator.

The reconciliation service. What should you do in that reconciliation service? I have hinted at some key things, but let me state them more clearly. You will want to: 1) do identificational repentance as both pastor and boards, seeking forgiveness from the congregation and from God; 2) allow time for response; 3) establish some symbols or take some symbolic actions (like the Lord's Table); and 4) commit yourselves together as leaders and congregation to move on to do what God wants you to do as a church.

First, in identificational repentance, you will speak to the congregation standing in the place of the previous pastor or pastors who may have hurt them. Your role as pastor permits this identification and your own sinful heart and/or temptations form the basis for sincerity of confession. This is not fun. You have to wait for the fun. The Divine Physician is doing His surgery. This is the healthy kind of pain, the kind that leads to healing. You use your mediatorial authority to bear this. The earlier in your ministry tenure this occurs the easier it is. That way you may not have a load of pain inflicted by this congregation upon you to process.

Following you, and perhaps more painfully, are the appointed spiritual lay leaders of the church. It is more painful because they were actually there and guilty (although most people would not hold them as guilty). It is the job of the shepherds to protect the sheep from wolves, even those wolves that arise from among the leaders themselves (John 10:11-15; Acts 20:28-30). Therefore the failure to protect the congregation from an abusive despot is their responsibility. I hope that working through the history of the church will make this failure evident. You will need your courageous leaders to stand and take responsibility for the failures and seek forgiveness of the congregation. The courage it takes to do this will enhance their leadership standing. People will recognize it. Such confessions should be formally written out and read. The speakers can then add extemporaneously to these formal comments should they wish to do so.

Second, there should be a time for response from the congregation, but such response should not be coerced or manipulated. Nor is it even necessary. The symbolic action of leadership and the communion that follows will be enough for people to lay their grudges and painful memories down. However, it is appropriate to extend an opportunity for verbal acceptance of the confessions and to grant forgiveness as long as people feel there is no obligation to say anything.

You need to make this freedom perfectly clear. *Chances are some will speak as long as they have the freedom not to do so.* You never want to force forgiveness out of an abused individual. Part of the healing from abuse is the freedom to forgive when someone is ready to do so. This is true for congregations as well. When they do forgive, there is likely to be a release of strong emotions, of grief and sorrow. You should be ready for these powerful emotions and not be afraid of them. Such emotions are a part of healing from abuse and their presence is evidence of that healing.

Third, establish some symbols of the event. God loves symbols and fills the Scriptures with them. Minimally, the Lord's Table is always appropriate in this context. Closing the service with Communion can be enormously powerful and healing. In a sense *we ingest the antidote to our own brokenness*—the broken body and shed blood of the Savior. He forgives sin and heals the wounded heart. Emphasize the *corporate significance* of Communion, not just the individual significance. Christ binds the congregation to Himself and each other by remembering what He has done, not just for me as an individual but for us as a body. If you have taught the concept of the church's corporate heart, then this is the time to apply it.

Other symbols may work here as well. I remember doing a foot washing for a Bible study I had when I was in college as a symbol of servanthood. There are not many contexts where it would be appropriate, but this is one where it could be. You could wash the feet of the board members as a symbol of the servant nature of true biblical authority. The danger is in the "showiness" of it—you must do it with the proper motivation.

Another possibility of symbolic action is the re-establishing of committee leaders or groups the former pastor may have eliminated. As mentioned, abusive pastors often will stop any ministry they can not personally attend or lead. Recommissioning such groups and their leaders as a part of this service may have a wonderful impact.

Pray for some God-designed symbols. Allow the Spirit to guide your heart and creativity to them. A plaque or a banner with an appropriate verse could stand as a symbol. Hang it in a conspicuous place permanently. "The Son of Man didn't come to be served but to serve," (Mark 10:45) might send the right message. "I came that they might have life, and might have it abundantly," (John 10:10) or "The good shepherd lays down his life for the sheep," (John 10:11) are two other possibilities to remind the church of the nature of true spiritual authority. A plaque or banner of "By His wounds, you are healed" (1 Peter 2:24) likewise would stand as a constant reminder of what had taken place on your "Reconciliation Sunday."

Fourth, after the Communion it is crucial to have a time of committal, of dedication to close the service. In the shadow of the Lord's Table, you and the board members should publicly rededicate yourselves to Christ to serve and bless your church, to lead it with wisdom and love. The congregation should dedicate themselves to pray for all the leaders. You might ask some key non-board members to come and lay hands on all of you and pray, or give a general invitation for anyone to stand and pray for the leadership. All these actions reconnect the heart of the congregation with the heart of the leaders, and in so doing heal the corporate heart of the church.

"Will this really work?" you wonder. I can guarantee that it will help more than ignoring the damage done by the previous ministry. One of the great lies we have been told in our generation is that time heals all wounds. It does not! Indeed by God's design it does not. Such a statement *attributes to time what only the work of Christ can accomplish.* The proactive role of mediatorial authority in exercising their God-given authority under Christ can heal the ancient wounds. Such work is hard and humbling. Such work carries no guarantees, but you are proclaiming nothing but truth by the symbolic actions we have suggested. Those who have ears to hear what the Spirit is saying to your church will hear and respond.

Summary. Pastors who abuse churches and church members are quite common and create one of the most difficult wounds in a church's heart to heal. A church with an abusive pastor in its history is apt to demonstrate several dysfunctional characteristics: 1) dependent people; 2) weak lay leaders; 3) a repressed or rigid atmosphere.

Healing has a chance of happening though identificational repentance, both by the pastor before the boards, and by the pastor and boards before the church. You will want to create a reconciliation service filled with symbols reflecting true servant leadership and the power of Christ to heal the deepest wounds.

Chapter 11

*LEADING THE CONGREGATION TO HEALING: CHURCHES THAT ABUSE PASTORS**

I was driving somewhere and readied myself to make a left turn at a traffic light. What happened before and after this event, I have no idea, what happened next is crystal clear. A car drove up beside me with a burly man at the wheel. In the back seat a two or three year old boy was in a car seat. I glanced over to his car in time to see him lean back and wail on this toddler with the back of his huge hand, again and again. I was so shocked that I froze. One hundred things now flood my mind of what I could have/should have done, because what I did was nothing. The light changed and I made my turn, breathless, but nonetheless I turned away. If there is a motivation for writing this chapter, it is found in that memory.

I am a non-violent man by nature, but remembering that man pummeling that child fills me with wrath I find hard to contain. I understand Jesus' warning in Matthew 18 to those who cause one of His little children to stumble. Find a boulder, tie it around your neck, take a cruise and jump with the boulder into the Marianas Trench. You don't want to face God if you have done this! It encourages me to know my feelings are similar to God's on the subject. God is just.

Turn that burly man into a church and that child into a good-hearted pastor, and you get the picture I have seen more than I want to in my work with churches and friendships with pastors. There may not be a greater challenge on earth than working with an abuser, on any level. The mixture of emotions an abuser creates in a counselor makes the process of healing doubly difficult. Edwin Chase describes what he terms "radical evil" in the church.

> When we think of radical evil, our minds race toward scenes of genocide, torture, or some other massive abuse of power where

people are wounded or destroyed. The church on the corner with its gleaming steeple does not immediately come to mind. This blind spot is a major part of the problem. Most ministers and well-informed laypersons are not prepared for the outbreak of radical evil in the community of faith.

Recent surveys indicate that sixty-two percent of the pastors who have been forced to leave their churches were ousted by churches that had previously ousted one or more pastors. Ten percent of all U.S. churches have forced out three or more pastors. Chase appropriately calls these churches "repeat offenders."[iii] Add this to a survey done by Southern Baptists that revealed ninety percent of the laity claimed that the primary method of resolving a church conflict was to "fire the pastor."[iv]

I remember my friend John, forty-two years old, who was recuperating from a heart attack. He told me he could no longer preach with his glasses on.

"What do you mean?" I asked.

He replied, "I have people in my church who think I am preaching at them when I look at them. They know I am blind as a bat without my glasses."

My friends Richard and Garry pastored the same abusive church back to back. I remember Richard telling me that for seven years it was like he preached to a wall. Garry—such a gentle, kind man—was torn up emotionally by the experience and dropped out of ministry for a while. I remember feeling a sense of joy when I heard that church had closed its pastor-chewing doors. God is merciful.

I find it easier to identify with abused pastors than with abused churches. I know that many good brethren have been called to the opposite ministry, and I applaud them. I realize that both ministries reflect the heart concern of God for His hurting children. Their experience has prepared them for their ministry, as my experience has prepared me for mine. God is wise and good.

How does one go about addressing the enormous challenge of healing the heart of an abusive church? How do you, as a pastor, get a church to take responsibility for the hurtful ways it has dealt with its previous pastors and stand a chance of ensuring it might not happen to you? God will help you in the attempt. Believe me, He wants it to stop too.

THE NATURE OF CHURCHES THAT ABUSE

What is meant by the abuse of pastors? As with child abuse, there are numerous ways churches can abuse their shepherds. The abuse ranges from insensitivity to needs all the way to threats, lies, betrayal, and victimization in the public forum through charges and innuendoes. It is not possible to cover every single way churches can abuse their pastors, but some broad categories should help define it.

Repeat offender churches establish a pattern of abuse, devastating a string of pastors one after the other. Because pastors, especially those fresh out of seminary or with little church experience, are naïve about how to assess a church before they accept a call, they walk innocently into these destructive situations. They don't talk to the former pastors to find out what happened. If they do talk to them, they don't ask the right questions. They accept the word of the search committee that the problem lay with the former pastor(s). "But it will be different with you," they assure him. "You are a different kind of person." The truth is nothing has changed in the church.

So you have taken a new church. What are the warning signs to alert you that your church has abused previous pastors?

Insensitivity and neglect. Many children are abused inadvertently out of insensitivity and neglect of their needs. Pastors experience the same abuse. In our first church, we were barely paid a living wage. I was fresh out of seminary and find it difficult to ask for money anyway (like my father who had trouble asking for what he needed), so I never spoke up when I should have. Every year the church would vote on my salary and haggle over the minuscule increases they gave me. No one ever came and asked what we needed. My wife and I looked around our home and realized that almost every piece of furniture we had was a gift from family. Our cars were gifts from our family. We would not have been able to afford any of it otherwise. It would be one thing if the congregation was poor and I was called to be poor among them. This was not the case. Most of the people in our church lived comfortably, owned their homes, had two cars, and an RV.

It is neither evil nor wrong to ask for what you need. Coward that I was, it wasn't until I left the church that I was able to communicate to friends on the boards that the situation had been unlivable. To their credit they apologized to my wife and me, and made sure they paid the subsequent pastors better. If you have the courage up front to talk about what you need, good for you. However, if during your research of the history of your church, you discover that they have not taken care of a previous pastor or pastors, you may want to lead the church to apologize and make restitution in some fashion. Such a public action could heal the heart of an insensitive church.

Insensitive leaders fail to appreciate the burdens that a pastor bears. Few people realize the kinds of issues and pressure that are a regular part of ministry. Not only is there a total lack of awareness of how long it takes to prepare a fresh sermon, most people have no idea that pastors, like doctors, are on call 24/7, 365 days a year. After years of ministry, the pressure is routine. You are no longer aware of the pressure when someone calls in the middle of the night because a group of church teens were in a serious auto accident; or someone's mother is taking her last breaths and they want you there on Thanksgiving Day, derailing your own family preparations.

Then there are those who are angry with you because of what psychologists call *transference* and *projection*. In transference, people transfer onto you their angry feelings about people in authority who have hurt them. In projection, they project upon you an image of what they need you to be for them. When you fall short, they are ripped at you. Another form of projection is when people project their own feelings onto you and presume you feel like they do. So if they are unloving, they will accuse you of being unloving; if they feel guilty, they will project guilt upon you and will be suspicious that you have done something terrible. By bringing down someone "higher than they are," they alleviate their guilt.

Pastors always have a segment of their congregations who are hurting and struggling with these issues. What they need are church lay leaders who are sensitive to the pressures and demands of such "invisible" things beyond the normal "visible" pressures of preaching, leading the church's growth, and maintaining a healthy marriage and family. The comment "It must be nice to work just one hour a week" can hurt if a pastor feels such insensitivity. When there is no sensitivity to these pressures or any allowance given in extra vacation time or sabbaticals, pastors can begin to feel a toxic loneliness or burnout. I see this as a form of abusive neglect and insensitivity. A church with a history like this can be led to see the light. Most will respond if they realize what they are doing. A survey of the church's history and into reasons why pastors have left could open their eyes and hearts.

Controllers. Up the scale from the insensitive are the controlling. Controlling people have a scale of severity all their own. They have been described vividly by other writers: Marshall Shelley calls them *Well-intentioned Dragons* (Bethany House, 1994); Leith Anderson introduces us to the controlling "Ralph" in *Dying for Change* (Bethany House, 1998), and M. Scott Peck describes sinister controllers who crush the spiritual life of others in *People of the Lie* (Touchstone, 1998). Controllers vary in degrees of willfulness, motivation, and premeditation, but their impact can be deadly to a minister at any level.

The severity of the abuse depends on the positions from which these controlling people operate, how much power and/or support they have, and how open they are to learn and change. Often they are carrying deep wounds from either authority figures of their past (transference), or specifically from previous pastors or spiritual leaders. They harbor mistrust rooted in pain that expresses itself in a defensive, controlling, hostile attitude.

I saw this firsthand when the leaders of a nearby church asked me to mediate a church discipline meeting. The members at the center of the issue were an older couple who had been resistant and hostile to every pastor who came to the church. They were classic controllers with a predictable pattern. Whenever a new pastor and his wife arrived, this couple would ingratiate themselves to them. There is a pastoral proverb every candidate should remember: "Beware of the man who first picks you up at the airport or who wants you to stay in his home." Such individuals usually have an agenda, and want to be the first church members to "plant their seeds" in the ear of the potential new pastor.

In this case, the husband was a gifted musician and song leader—he made sure the new pastor knew that up front. In the months that followed, the new pastor would often call upon this man to lead the worship service. With more and more authority the worship leader heavy-handedly imposed his will over the musical styles, the soloists, the instrumentalists, and the people who were permitted to minister. He alienated many members along the way. Life became increasingly miserable for the pastor. This pattern of hostility went back *forty years* (!) to a time when a pastor was responsible for hurting this couple badly. They had made life miserable for pastor after pastor for forty years. To this church's credit, during an interim period between pastors, the board members finally addressed this historical evil.

Sometimes there are double issues to be addressed. Another pastor told me of the hostile control of the principal of the Christian school attached to his church. This man had supported the founding pastor some thirty years before when the pastor was accused of immorality. He stuck his neck out to defend this pastor publicly because he believed the charges were false. The charges turned out to be true and the pastor left in disgrace (an issue affecting the corporate heart). However, this principal, who admitted he felt totally betrayed, stayed. It is not hard to imagine how much he distrusted pastors after that kind of betrayal. Perhaps if the church leaders had done identificational repentance about that original pastor's immorality, they could have helped this individual let go of his bitterness. Hard to say, but either way, the leaders needed to address both issues—the original pastor's immorality and the controller's ongoing resistance.

Jesus speaks to the corporate body in Thyatira and describes their responsibility for a controlling woman among them, "You (sing.) *permit* the woman Jezebel, who calls herself a prophetess, to teach and seduce my servants" (Revelation 2:20). This is not as much about gender ("Jezebel" is clearly a symbolic name) as it is about someone in a power position who influences people to do evil. Jesus' rebuke to the church (singular) is that *they permit this*. If a new pastor does a historical review and lets the leadership educate him in the history, doubtless some stories of crises and pain will revolve around the controlling behavior of such individuals. Why? Jesus inflicts the church of Thyatira with pain to get them to take action.

And I gave her time to repent of her sexual immorality, and she didn't repent. Indeed I will *cast her into a sickbed*, and those who commit adultery with *her into great tribulation*, unless they repent of their deeds. I *will kill her children with death*, and all the churches shall know that I am He who searches the minds and hearts. And I will give to each one of you according to your works. (2:21-23)

The symbolic language of Revelation is not as crucial here as much as the recognition that pain and loss are the main forms of divine communication if there has been no repentance. It is the controller and the followers who must repent in this case. Leaders must recognize their responsibility to deal with the controlling individuals and not be intimidated.

Churches with controlling people undergo pain and crises continually. Just like families that have abusers in them, getting unstuck from the morass and changing the system is a challenge! For one thing, such people are probably *sitting around the table* sharing the history of the church with the pastor. If they are not there, some of their followers or friends probably are. They often have leadership positions. They won't necessarily go quietly into the night, but they need to recognize the source of their pain and repent.

Snipers. Snipers are people who regularly engage in non-constructive criticism that often moves into gossip and rumor-mongering, the "Monday-morning quarterbacks" of the church. They are not interested in power; they won't give controllers any competition. They tend to stay hidden and shoot at the pastor from concealed positions. They usually feel marginalized in the church; they feel that they have no voice in what happens. Where every church has a sniper or two, abusive churches have a battalion, indiscriminate of gender, age, or education. They take their unhappiness with specific things and distribute it like ammo out to the rest of the battalion.

When a pastor has trouble with conflict, snipers are empowered. No one shoots back! They will leave the Sunday service and go out to lunch together to "discuss" the latest perceived heresy in the sermon or horror in the service. The pastor finds this out when there are disgusted non-snipers among them who report it to him. This negativity and criticism can become devastating to pastors.

Snipers are used to this backstage approach to conflict. Many have been well trained in it. They do it in their families too. They talk about the problems they have with members of the family with everyone but the member with whom they have the problem. Snipers camouflage themselves as faithful church members because they would not miss a service or business meeting. All the while they gather intelligence on their target. Their feeling of ownership of the church is high even though they feel marginalized. I had a sniper tell me once, "We will be here a long time after you leave, pastor." If a pastor confronts a sniper about their gossip, they are highly offended and that confrontation adds to their arsenal. They would never feel what they do is gossiping. They express "concern for the church." This concern is seldom expressed directly to the leadership in a forum to discuss it or resolve it as constructive criticism should be.

Sometimes snipers will attend business meetings and read letters (as the one I described earlier). In this setting they feel empowered as they question the proposals of the leadership. They may have had the business meeting agenda weeks before, but they don't bring their concerns to the leaders privately. They wait to voice it publicly where it cannot be discussed properly or without emotion. I agree that people *should voice* disagreements; it is when it is *always the same people* and everyone *knows* they will say something to raise the tension of the meeting that you recognize a sniper in your midst. Invariably they claim "a lot of people [none of whom are at the meeting] have come to me" and "everyone is unhappy." Their modus operandi is to produce a negative, tense atmosphere that wears a pastor down. If there are enough snipers, a dark cloud of negativity can settle over church services. It is only a matter of time before there is a major discharge.

Snipers can be exposed. A key to discerning them is defining those things that cause them to feel marginalized and addressing them. We saw a significant number of our snipers (many of whom were in the choir) become supporters when we gave the choir a prominent role in our reconciliation process. In a deliberate move, I joined the choir for a Christmas cantata during this period. That really helped. Symbolic moves such as this can lessen the number of snipers. You never eliminate them completely; some remain to keep you humble.

Wounded bears. Some people who abuse pastors are hard to categorize. We've looked at how some controllers have been wounded and seek power. There is another group of the walking, worshiping wounded, however, who are irrational, obsessed, or just plain weird. I choose to call these people "wounded bears." Many of them suffer from a wide variety of psychological illnesses—borderline personality, bipolar disorder, schizophrenia, obsessive-compulsive disorder to name a few—and God in His grace has called them to Himself. Nevertheless, they remain needy and troubled, and can be a boatload of trouble to a vulnerable pastor.

Dealing with wounded bears requires pastoral diligence, patience and leadership sensitivity. They can take up an enormous amount of a pastor's time and energy. At times they are downright dangerous. They are apt to attack without provocation, or they see/hear/sense slights and injury where there are none and attack. Some hold the pastor responsible for their own misery, struggles and pain. Any number of things could be the cause of their present misery: the pastor, his counsel, his latest sermon, or an illustration he gave in that sermon. Though wounded bears may have a history of such claims against authority figures, they can accuse an innocent pastor of doing things to them, saying things about them, touching them inappropriately, abusing them secretly. They may even blackmail the pastor with threats about going public with such charges. Some are so psychologically damaged that sometimes they fabricate or rewrite events in their minds and believe their fantasies.

God forbid that any pastor genuinely guilty of such abuse should escape detection. If he escapes from human justice, he won't escape divine recompense. However, having pastored for twenty-three years, I have encountered a wide variety of wounded bears, been attacked by some and threatened by others. I know what they are capable of doing. Unfortunately, we live in a day when such accusations are believed first and have to be disproved. Some are hard to disprove, even for a pastor with integrity. I had a woman with a voyeuristic older brother once say to me, "You are looking at me exactly the way my brother looked at me!" How do I disprove that? There are godly pastors who are victims of such injustice, who have had good ministries destroyed due to false accusations. The church's heart is wounded by such events.

If there has been such an episode in the history of your church, the healing process needs to be done at the leadership level. Never make such a process public, both for the sake of the wounded person, their family, and others who would not understand. This healing process needs to be done among the previous pastor, the present pastor, and the board members in *confidence and privacy*. Board members utilizing their mediatorial authority can stand in the place of the congregation to confess the injustice done to the pastor and seek his forgiveness. This might not set the public record straight but would go a long way toward healing the hurt of the previous pastor. The leadership could also offer to act as references for the previous pastor if he wants to find a new ministry.

Organized resistance or rebellion. Most of the people described so far operate as individuals. Their numbers may be large enough to form a significant percentage of the congregation at times, they may talk to each other, but usually they are not *organized*. They don't meet and discuss strategy about what they will do to resist the initiatives or direction of the pastor or church. Sometimes though, if problems are not addressed, if conflicts stay underground long enough, a polarizing event can cause opposition to galvanize and get organized.

Any church that has had a petition passed or a meeting held in someone's home with a single agenda item—"What to do about the pastor"—has had organized rebellion. If the pastor is abusive himself, people may feel that such a meeting is the only means of circumventing his power and control. However, it is an act of significant distrust in appointed leadership, even if that leadership is not worthy of trust. As such, it still creates a wound in a church's heart even if people felt it was their only option.

In many cases though, the pastor has *not* been abusive. Most commonly they accuse him of leading the church in an "unhealthy" or "destructive" direction. In our present church culture this means he may have attempted to lead the church ministry out of a traditional style of worship and ministry into a more contemporary style, but the issues are constantly changing. The controversy used to be centered on the overhead projector ("When the overhead projector goes on, the Holy Spirit goes out!"). Now it is PowerPoint® and the computer projection system. It is the new choruses, the drums, the guitars, the hymnbook that remains closed in the pew. The pastor uses the NIV or The Message or anything other than the King James. People just don't like change!

Church members have a terrible history of demonizing and devil-making their pastors and each other in order to maintain a "status quo." They are uncomfortable with changes taking place, so they find a "spiritual reason" to justify their emotional discomfort. They sift a pastor's sermons for doctrinal content, and invariably they find some "dangerous" doctrine. "He is too charismatic/Calvinistic/Arminian/liberal. The New Age/Feminists/Modern psychology/The social gospel has corrupted him." When times were good, the pastor's emphasis was not problematic. Not so now. Unhappy congregants scrutinize sermons for inappropriate illustrations and humor. The pulpit, they decide, is "not holy" anymore.

They examine the pastor's schedule and find he (is/is not) spending (enough/too much) time doing (visiting/counseling/praying/evangelizing/ etc.). God obviously (is not blessing him/has deserted him/was never with him) because of this.

His leadership style comes under fire. He is too (weak/authoritarian/controlling/insipid/laid back). He does not keep his staff under control or he controls his staff too much and they "hate working for him." Any recent conflict or problem with a staff person is exaggerated to prove the pastor is unable to lead. Any past mistake or misjudgment is further proof of his incompetence.

When opposition gets organized, they begin to recruit people. Petitions are passed, worded in ways to maximize the number of people willing to sign it. Often an unhappy staff person is recruited, and sometimes will even lead the rebellion. This is as old as Moses. If a board member has a problem with the pastor or the direction he is leading the church, they enlist him to add credibility to the rebellion.

When a rebellion gets organized, anything in the pastor's life becomes fair game. His wife, his marriage, his children, his hobbies, his extra-curricular activities, the car he drives (too nice/an embarrassment), the clothes he wears (I remember one pastor who got criticized for wearing pastel shirts!), are all targets. When you have to turn someone God has called to your church into a demon, you must find *lots* of evidence.

This is flat-out abuse. It is hard to believe that Christians will do this to Christians. I grieve for the many good men who have experienced it while helping a church adjust its ministry to relate to contemporary culture. It is true that Old Testament prophets and even the Lord Jesus experienced such abuse during their ministries (for a lot of the same reasons). That fact doesn't make the injury to both the heart of the pastor and the heart of the church today any less devastating.

No church can do this to their pastor and remain healthy. Even if it's not evident, a climate of distrust fills the church. A new pastor's "honeymoon" with a church is a dangerous illusion. It makes the ultimate conflict even more hurtful because of the vulnerability and hope it creates. Pastors are never perfect and change management is risky. When the honeymoon is over, something can and will happen to trigger another rebellion. Such attitudes and patterns get locked into the heart of the church until they are resolved.

HEALING THE HEART OF YOUR CHURCH

Understanding reconciliation in this context. Reconciliation in a church that has had organized rebellions requires bold but careful action on the part of the church leadership. If your church has a history of abusing its pastors this way, don't believe it will be different for you as pastor. If you are a lay leader reading this, you bear significant responsibility for healing this sinful behavior that has affected the heart of your church, otherwise *the pattern will be repeated*. The lay leadership must *take responsibility* for the injuries that have been perpetrated against pastors under their watch. The leadership also needs to act together to confront instigators and organizers of the rebellion(s) if they are still around.

The leadership needs to do an honest and fair assessment of the ministries of the previous pastors. For if a church has abused the pastors God sent, in any way, even if they were not perfect, there will be major corporate heart issues with God, the kinds of things that won't allow a church to grow or prosper. The following questions need to be answered with prayerful sensitivity to what God is trying to teach the church.

1. Is the church presently not reconciled with any of its previous pastors? Why?
2. Were the pastors as evil as they were portrayed? Were any of them "demonized" undeservedly?
3. Were their ministries as bad as everyone seemed to feel or were faults exaggerated in order to justify rejection of those ministries?
4. Was the issue pastoral insensitivity rather than unspirituality, a lack of wisdom rather than a lack of holiness, personality rather than ungodliness, style rather than false doctrine, lack of experience rather than lack of competence?
5. Did things that were said or done unjustifiably hurt any of the pastor's family members?
6. Did the lay leadership of that time appropriately assess the pastor's ministry or did it allow majority opinion, the threats of major contributors, or the loudest voices to sway its decision-making?
7. Did any pastor leave "under a cloud," with unresolved issues with the church because of the way he felt he was treated? How much responsibility does the leadership honestly bear for that "cloud," for being unable or unwilling to work out those issues with the pastor?
8. Did the leadership handle the conflict around the pastor's leaving well or poorly? If poorly, what could they have done differently?

Needless to say, such a soul-searching analysis by church leadership takes enormous spiritual courage. However, if you want to be the kind of leaders God can bless and have the kind of church God can fulfill His purposes in, nothing less than ruthless honesty will do.

"But," someone will counter, "the pastor did this and said this and preached this! We were not wrong in removing him!" The pastor may indeed have demonstrated "sinful reactivity" to being attacked or to having his family attacked. Often people will use such reactions to justify false or exaggerated accusations after the fact. "See," the perpetrators gloat, "we *told* you he was ungodly!" I had a pastor tell me once that a woman would provoke him to the point of anger by insulting him, his ministry and his family, and then she would say "See! You have an anger problem."

The pastor may have words, actions, and reactions for which he needs to take responsibility in order to repent, reconcile completely and clear his own conscience. He may be so hurt he is unwilling to reconcile. *The projected response of the former pastor can not be the concern of the leadership in this analysis.* They also must resist all attempts to self-justify the actions or failures that may have been abusive to the pastor. They must instead take responsibility for their shortcomings alone.

Peter looked at John in John 21 and had the temerity to ask Jesus, "What about this man?" "What is that to you?" Jesus challenged him (and us), "You follow Me!" What John does, says, or does not do is not Peter's concern. God will deal with the former pastor in a similar manner. *Our issue is to determine what God is saying to our leadership and our church and to act upon it.* We need to determine what has affected the heart of our church before God. Is there any failure of the leadership to do what it should have done?

Two levels to reconciliation. There are two levels to reconciliation—the divine and the human—illustrated in Matthew 5:23-24 and Romans 12:28. Jesus says in Matthew: *"Therefore if you bring your gift to the altar, and there remember that your brother has something against you, leave your gift there before the altar, and go your way. First be reconciled to your brother, and then come and offer your gift."* God stresses the importance of doing the horizontal work of reconciliation with our brother before we can experience the acceptance of whatever we offer vertically to God. However, Matthew 5 assumes that our brother will want to be reconciled with us. Sometimes that is not the case. I once worked with a church where the pastor and his wife had been so hurt, he refused to accept a phone call from anyone belonging to the church's leadership.

What do you do if the pastor who had been abused does not want to talk, does not accept the repentance of the leadership, or their offer to make things right?

1. You can not allow an initial rebuff to put you off. After a hostile first conversation it is quite easy to say, "Well, we tried," shrug your shoulders, and walk away. Not so fast! The responsibility goes deeper than that. I believe in the case where the leadership feels convicted that the church has treated a pastor badly/abusively, there is a debt to be paid. Not a monetary debt (though in some cases that may also be appropriate), but an obligation

to keep trying to make things right. Abused people often react badly when the perpetrator or their representatives come around. They feel vulnerable and unsafe. It opens the wound again. You have to accept that first rebuff and try again.

2. If you can not make positive contact, ask a mediator to step in, someone who has a relationship both with your church and the pastor, but someone whom the pastor trusts. This could be another local pastor, a superintendent of the denomination, or a third party of the pastor's choosing. Explain to the mediator what you have discovered in the historical analysis, how God has spoken to you about it and what you are trying to do to make things right. Tell the mediator that you are not asking anything of the pastor except the chance to repent and make amends if possible. This must be true. The pastor may have things he needs to repent for as well, but let the mediator assure him that this process is not about him. If you focus on what he has done to justify the church's actions or attitudes, you will never get it right with God. *You are working solely on what the church must do through its mediatorial leaders to get right with God.* The mediator can carry this message and bring back a reply. Hopefully this will facilitate communication. However, what if this attempt also breaks down? (I have been the mediator in such an episode).

3. Write a corporate letter (one from the leaders on behalf of the congregation) of confession and send it with a significant gift (see Proverbs 18:16; 21:14). This action will get attention and help soothe some of the hurt. It will show how serious you are about making things right. This may not be an easy sell to the church leaders, especially if the pastor or pastors have already given them a couple of hostile rebuffs. But it is critical that you persevere. Here is a sample letter:

Dear Pastor Jackson,

We want you to understand the reason for the attached check of $1000. Writing a letter like this is one of the most difficult things we have ever had to do as church leadership here at First Bible Church, but coming to realize how badly we have hurt you and your family grieves us so much, we have no choice before God. We understand why you might not want to hear from us, but we pray you will read the following with an open heart.

We need to share with you a little of how God has spoken to us in recent months. In an effort to see how God wants to direct our church in the future, we have prayerfully analyzed our past church history to see what God has been saying to us. We believe

He has spoken to us about the way we treated you when you were here at First Bible. We know that was ten years ago now and you may have left that chapter of your history behind you. We, however, feel the divine burden of conviction that the things said about you and done to you and your family at that time were never made right.

As the present church leadership, we want to take responsibility for those things, some of which we mention:

The failure to protect you and your family from abusive and destructive criticism. We take responsibility for letting some in the congregation continue to batter you with unfair criticism. They should have been stopped and disciplined, and we failed to do so. There were board members at that time that participated in the criticism too. They likewise should have been rebuked. Their actions were neither godly nor good.

The lack of support when you were obviously hurting. Instead of coming alongside you and being supportive during that difficult time, we take responsibility for deserting you and leaving you alone to face those conflicts. We said little or nothing when you were being attacked.

The petition that was passed and the meetings that were organized by people attempting to remove you should have been stopped. We take responsibility for failing to work with you to resolve those congregational conflicts in a godly, orderly manner. As leaders charged by God with the management of the household of God, we failed God, you and the church by not doing our job. We were part of the problem instead of part of the solution. God has spoken to us about how many times in our history we have failed to facilitate healthy communication in times of conflict. We are working to correct that now.

As a congregation, we allowed you to leave First Bible with a great deal of hurt in your heart and discouragement about the ministry God called you to do. We never should have allowed that to happen. We know it took you three years afterwards to even want to go back into pastoral ministry and we feel responsible for those years.

We write this so you will know and understand that we take full responsibility for the failures and sins of the past leadership and repent before you. We ask you to forgive the church and us. God has disciplined us severely over this, and we need to make things right if we can. The $1,000 is a very small token of this desire, but the best that we can do at the moment. Please accept it as such. We know that money does not alone resolve a heart issue, but we hope that it will provide some proof of the sincerity of our hearts. Is there anything you would feel we could do to make restitution for what you lost as a result of your time at First Bible? If it is within our power, we will do it.

Sincerely in Christ,
The Boards of First Bible Church

"Wouldn't such admissions make you libel for a lawsuit?" you might ask. Yes, such admissions do render a church vulnerable. An angry pastor could decide to become vengeful and take a church to court. That could happen anyway, but when will believers stop worrying about human courts and start worrying about the only Judge whose verdict matters? I am aware that a possible lawsuit might stop a church from going as far as it needs to make things right with God's servants it has hurt—and am horrified by the cowardice behind it!

Reconciliation rebuffed. The majority of pastors are going to respond to this kind of sincere attempt to reconcile, usually with the first contact. Most will understand the spiritual significance of refusing to do so. However, I have met some pastors that were so enraged by what a church had done to them, even years after the events, that I am not certain any reconciliation attempt would be successful. God calls us to forgive those who trespass against us, but we all know how difficult that is when someone has deeply wounded us.

Dallas Willard describes such a situation in Matthew 5:

Of course the legalistic tendency in the human self will immediately go to work. It never seems to rest. It will ask, What if my brother refuses to be reconciled? Am I never to go to church again? ("First be reconciled to your brother and then come offer your gift.") Do I always have to do this, no matter what else is at issue in the situation? The answer is, Obviously not! Jesus is not here giving a law that you must never carry through with your religious practice if an associate has something against you. He is not stating a law like "Thou shalt not kill." *The aim of his illustration—and it is an illustration—is to bring us to terms with what is in our hearts and, simultaneously, to show us the rightness of the kingdom heart.* (Italics mine)

He goes on to say:

> We don't control outcomes and are not responsible for them, but only for our contribution to them. Does our heart long for reconciliation? Have we done what we can? Honestly? Do we refuse to substitute ritual behaviors for genuine acts of love? *Do we mourn the harm that our brother's anger is doing to his own soul, to us, and to others around us? If so, we are beyond "the righteousness of the scribes and Pharisees" and immersed in God's ways.*[vi] (Italics mine)

When has a church or church leadership done enough to be free of past abuse? When they have honestly tried at *least* the three steps above. If no attempts are successful, their church is able to go to God with a clean conscience. God does not bind us if a person won't forgive us when we have sincerely confessed—*that becomes a problem of the one failing to forgive.* We cannot control what they do, nor can we make them forgive us. However, we must make a sincere effort to reconcile, even if they choose not to forgive. Paul says in Romans 12:18 *"If it is possible, as much as depends on you, live peaceably with all men."* The key here is the "as much as depends on you." You must give it more than a weak attempt. You must work to break through the walls of hurt that the abuse may have erected with the knowledge it may fail. It is nevertheless important to do.

If you come to the end of the process with one of the injured pastors unwilling to forgive, you can (and should) "mourn the harm" that his anger is doing to his own soul. Then you can move on and leave him to God.

Reconciliation accepted. If the pastor is gracious and accepts the offer of reconciliation, he may take the opportunity to own up to the things for which he feels responsible in what went wrong and ask forgiveness of the church. If this is the case, inviting him back for a service of public confession and forgiveness by both sides may be appropriate. If he agrees to come, you could plan a joint service of reconciliation. The congregation could be primed with a series of messages on the importance of repentance and forgiveness on the human level in order to be right with God.

As with a split, you could invite back people who had left the church or who had specific problems with the pastor and encourage them to reconcile with him. You could even give him the opportunity to speak. The more mutual ministry that occurs, the more healing can take place. Give him a chance to "leave" the church differently than he left before. The church should also be generous in facilitating his stay (if he is from out-of-town) and in his honorarium. All such details will be restorative. A church will never go broke being generous to God's servants.

By these actions, the leadership not only heals the heart of the church, but also repairs the heart of the pastor(s). The overall effect on the Body of Christ is overwhelmingly positive. The church will be ready to get on with the forward looking, visionary work it should do, and the Lord of the Church will facilitate it.

Summary. Sadly, there are pastors who abuse their churches, and there are also churches that abuse their pastors. Such abuse occurs in a variety of ways, including: insensitivity and neglect (where the needs of the pastor are not recognized or met); controllers, (who, having been wounded by authority or previous pastors, seek a "hostile takeover" to protect themselves); snipers, (who destructively criticize the ministry of the pastor); wounded bears, (people who have deep psychological problems); and, finally, an organized rebellion that results in the pastor leaving under duress.

If, in the review of your church's history, the church leadership finds indications of pastors who were abused, it needs to use its mediatorial authority to take steps to reconcile with these injured servants of God. Go as far as you possibly can to reconcile. If he is unwilling to be reconciled, you can mourn, but then know that God releases you and it has become his problem. Your church is cleansed of conscience. God does not bind you by a lack of forgiveness on the victim's part. If he is willing to be reconciled, you can have a service of reconciliation, and then get on with what God has called your church to do.

Chapter 12

LEADING THE CONGREGATION TO HEALING:
SINFUL REACTIVITY

We have all probably learned about the escalating spiral of violence in elementary school: Tom flicks a spit wad at Mike. Mike reaches over and punches Tom in the shoulder; not hard but hard enough. Tom, rubbing his shoulder, ups the ante—he punches Mike back harder. Mike, temper rising (he didn't hit Tom that hard) intentionally turns and kicks Tom in the shin. Within a minute, they're on the verge of a down and out brawl!

THE NATURE OF SINFUL REACTIVITY

This story illustrates what I call "sinful reactivity." I use the term "reactivity" instead of "reactions" because reactivity involves *potential* as well as actual reactions. Humans, from Cain on, have a difficult time keeping control of their reactions to a perceived provocation. The tempers of certain people can escalate quickly and lash out inappropriately, thus they are more "reactive." In a church environment, if the pastor feels he is tiptoeing through a minefield when he addresses a particular issue, it is because he recognizes that his congregation has a high level of "reactivity" to the subject.

In Israel, God managed this tendency to escalate reactions to a provocation by *lex talonis*, or the law of equal retaliation—"an eye for an eye"(Deut. 19:14-21). Unfortunately, this simple, direct way of enforcing justice is seldom utilized. Jesus made major modifications to the "eye for an eye" principle (Matt. 5:38-42). His changes are radically unpopular. He presented the idea of non-retaliation to a provocation. It boils down to this: if someone slaps you on the right cheek, you should let go of the idea of retaliation. The "requirements" of justice don't need to control your response. Jesus teaches us that retaliation is not our only option. We can resist the temptation to escalate the "violence;" we can even de-escalate it.

What does "control of response" mean? We go the second mile, take the second slap to demonstrate that our oppressor's provocation has not succeeded in controlling our heart response. You can say, "He has not made me angry; I have not let him go into my heart and push my anger button." You have removed from him the power to do so, proving it by your response. Peter tells us this is how Jesus suffered:

> To this you were called, because Christ suffered for you, leaving you an example, that you should follow in his steps. He committed no sin, and no deceit was found in his mouth. *When they hurled their insults at him, he didn't retaliate; when he suffered, he made no threats. Instead, he entrusted himself to him who judges justly* (1 Pet. 2:21-23 NIV).

Jesus and Peter speak of individual controlled response, but it also applies corporately. For churches, as much trouble comes from group reactions to perceived provocation, as to anything else. Manageable situations escalate quickly out of control. When a church atmosphere is charged with tension and good will has been used up, it does not take much for groups to start reacting to other groups. I have been with many a board that, feeling embattled, refers to itself as "us" and the congregation as "them." I confess at times to feeling "us-them" divisions as staff against boards, staff against seniors, staff against the choir.

Evangelical churches are filled with issues that can create strong reactivity. One group perceives itself more "spiritual" because the opposing group is obviously "satanically influenced." If something like this gets insinuated, bad feelings begin to escalate. Once one has been accused of being a spawn of Satan or propagating Satan's message, doctrines, or practices, it is hard to feel warm, loving thoughts toward one's accusers. Within congregations these "us-them" polarities occur between a variety of groups. The following is an initial list of such groups and issues (you may add others):

1. Age (seniors vs. youth)
2. Economics (those in favor of expensive new pews vs. those who think the money should go to missions)
3. Music and worship style (speaks for itself)
4. Future plans (building a new building vs. not building)
5. Personality (those who like the new worship leader vs. those who don't)
6. Doctrinal positions (Calvinists vs. Arminians; Five-point Calvinists vs. Four-point Calvinists; Lordship vs. Free Grace; Charismatic vs. Non-charismatic)

7. Matters of conscience (home schooling vs. public schooling; alcohol consumption vs. abstinence)

John Kenneth Galbraith is credited with saying, "Faced with the choice of changing one's mind and proving there is no need to do so, almost everyone gets busy on the proof." When "us-them" corporate polarities start, reactivity increases between the polarized groups as they start to marshal proofs of why their position is correct and the others are wrong. While sanctifying their own position, they demonize the opposition. Things are suspected, said, claimed, threatened or done, in reaction to any perceived slight or injury coming from the opposing group.

Sometimes out of these conflicts splits occur. We have covered that eventuality in chapter 9. I want to look at a situation where such reactivity causes a wound in the church but not a split; a wound that, should it remain unhealed, continues to impact the heart of the church. These wounds can become "infected," spreading and enlarging the discontent and tension into other areas of the church body.

IDENTIFY THE INCIDENTS OF REACTIVITY

How do you lead your church to healing if it has had some major blow-ups? First, the blow-ups need to be clearly identified. They often become evident in the review of the church's history. If a crisis didn't result in a split, it often results in hurt feelings and things presumed, said, or done that are hurtful. These hurt feelings do not resolve themselves with time if the leaders do not address them.

The incidents with our choir illustrate this kind of problem. When, under the previous pastor, the new choir director wanted to have auditions, reactivity was high. Things were said and done that were devastatingly hurtful to her, not the least of which was the humiliation of having to be replaced a month after taking the ministry. No one left the church but the wound remained also. It festered for over ten years. The choir was a hot bed of discontented members.

This same choir director was targeted again when we started our second congregation. A number of our key musicians moved into that new congregation and I needed musical help with the mother congregation. I asked her if she would join me in planning worship services as well as play the piano. She agreed. We worked together to create some fresh services. The reaction was horrible. People who previously had a problem with her began to complain loudly again. This emotional turbulence came to a head in a business meeting where her husband and one of the complainers almost had a fist fight. I had to replace her yet again, another crushing humiliation for her.

Once again a pastor stuck her in a vulnerable position and then bailed on her when things got hot. Much to my surprise, she and her husband remained in the church. I truly don't know why. What I do know is that they both became key players in our church's ultimate healing and proof of the reality that God had healed our church's heart.

Look for hotspots. In Yellowstone National Park, Old Faithful rests over what is known as a geologic "hotspot." The magma under the earth's crust comes close to the surface, heating underground water to extreme temperatures that keep building pressure. The geyser releases the pressure in a spouting plume of scalding hot water. Churches have such "hotspots" too— groups that are known to be vocal complainers. Their anger runs close to the surface and pressure is released with small provocation. Often (frustratingly) this occurs on a regular church schedule. It can be patterned around the church calendar or around the cycle of a pastor's ministry (right after his honeymoon).

The problem with hotspots is that members begin to know what reaction the group will have. The tendency is to grow tolerant and fatalistic, falling back on the "It has always been like this," explanation. Long-term tolerance does not help matters; it makes it more difficult to address the issue(s). Our choir was such a hotspot. In our case the choir's attitude was healed in the midst of our dealing with the other larger issues around the split. If we had not had the "benefit" of the split to initiate healing, we would still have had to confront the choir. It also taught us that sometimes hotspots exist because larger issues have not been addressed.

Another hotspot in our church was the relationship between the congregation and the boards. At church business meetings, the room was sometimes full of unspoken suspicion and distrust. We had to apply another principle to deal with this problem.

What it's about is often not what it's about. In counseling there is a principle that says "What it's about is often not what it's about." This is especially true in issues resulting in anger. Anger is so dominating an emotion that it makes us forget what actually *caused* the anger. By their hostility, the polarized groups may be saying something far more significant to the leaders than whatever they are angry about. The anger may have resulted in some things that require forgiveness (a good example of this is Cain in Genesis 4), but the *original sources* of the anger need to be identified also. These sources of anger may include discomfort with changes, the feeling they are being marginalized, not listened to or valued, personality conflicts, control and ownership issues, any number of things, all of which may be rooted in the church's history.

The leaders must assess the history properly, for the sinful reactivity may be rooted in a past sinful act or wound caused by either a previous pastor or board. If so, then identificational repentance by the pastor or board members is in order. It is almost a reflex to blame others first for wrongdoing. The pastor and boards are not immune from reacting to the anger. In our church, the sinful reactivity stopped after we (the leadership) had taken responsibility for some of the hurtful things in our church history.

How does one discern what the anger is really about? God's questions to Cain are highly relevant. "Why are you angry?" (Gen. 4:6) The question assumes that there was a stimulus, a painful cause in Cain's heart or experience that has resulted in the anger. The anger is a response to pain in some other area. God asks a "therapeutic question" designed to make Cain "reflect." God knows why Cain is angry, but Cain must ponder it and discover the cause. Reflecting on what the anger is *really* about is the first step to solving the problem. The leaders need to address the hurts caused by anger, but also identify the root problem that caused the anger in the first place. Otherwise, expect another explosion to take place.

God's second question to Cain is also astute in dealing with anger: "Why has your countenance fallen?" (Gen. 4:6) This question leads Cain to reflect on the way he has chosen to *express* his anger. So God wants Cain to go to both sides of the anger—its cause and the way it expresses itself—in order to find a godly response to it. His counsel actually moves Cain away from the domination of the anger to consider the issues around it. There is now hope for Cain, a healthy way to deal with his anger.

HEALING THE HEART OF YOUR CHURCH
There is a right thing to do. For everyone who has said, "This situation is beyond hope!" there is a right response that can *change everything*! God tells Cain "If you do well, won't [your countenance] be lifted up?" (Gen. 4:7, NASV) The NIV says, "If you do what is right, will you not be accepted?" The point is that, in the midst of his anger, *there is a right thing he can do*! If Cain does it, everything will change. The challenge is to find the right thing, a challenge God leaves to Cain to find on his own. God does the same for us.

You are thinking: *Cain didn't respond too well to God's wise counsel.* You can't fault the Counselor or the counsel. Interestingly enough, God's success rate as a "wonderful counselor" is not all that impressive! Cain rises up and murders his brother. The truth is, you could get hammered (but hopefully not murdered) as you attempt to deal with the hotspot. The "right thing" won't be measured by the response of the ones with whom you are dealing. Look at Moses, Jeremiah, and others in the Bible who tried to deal with a hard-hearted group. Doing the right thing as leaders can't be measured by right responses on the part of those you are trying to lead. However, you must persevere.

You as church leaders have taken responsibility for your part, but perhaps the angry response of the congregation shows there is hurt and injury remaining, that the wound is still there. What do you do?

Consider calling a "solemn assembly." A few churches have "solemn assemblies" as a part of their church calendar. What is a solemn assembly or a "holy convocation"? It is a description of the Old Testament appointed feast when the people would come together to the temple to fast and pray, and then to feast (Ex.12:16; Lev. 23). The assemblies were usually a week long (as with Passover and the Feast of the Unleavened Bread). These Israelite "congregational meetings" focused the people of God on the issues that were on the heart of God. They were highly symbolic (in that many symbols accompanied the feast) and focused on where the congregation stood before God.

That is exactly the purpose you want a solemn assembly to serve for your church. Many pastors deliver a "state of the church address" the first week of January, and such a sermon could tie into a solemn assembly. You could meet every night, or selected nights. During that week, Scriptural messages could revolve around the single focus of repentance, but your objective is the review of the church's history, both the previous year and how it fits into the whole history of the church. Construct your messages to incorporate some of the lessons the leaders feel God has taught the church through its history—where it stands now and what it needs to do. Elaborate on the key stories that illustrate these divine lessons.

The role of speaker does not always have to fall on the pastor's shoulders. Ask long-time church leaders who are capable of communicating well and who understand the significance of what you are doing to participate. Don't approach this event haphazardly—prepare carefully and publicize it regularly in advance. Building suspense and/or interest about it makes people want to come and find out what is going to be said/done. Biblical solemn assemblies were filled with symbolic actions and events. It is important for you to prayerfully consider what symbols might send appropriate messages in your church and serve as permanent reminders of the actions you take.

Though a solemn assembly could be used to help heal any of the previous wounds in your church's heart I have discussed, it would be especially effective for the problem of sinful reactivity. If the message Christ has been speaking to your church through its pain has been about sharp conflicts and out-of-control anger, you can address these by your messages and lead people to repentance. Because you are dealing with this *corporately*, no individual names need to be mentioned.

If there has been painful conflict between the seniors and the youth over the style of music, that is what you address. If the conflict has been doctrinal, then an emphasis on "the mark of a Christian" from John 13:34-35 is appropriate. There should be clarity about the harm such division continues to cause the church. The messages should lead to a climax on the final night— a night full of symbolic actions.

Involve connected leaders and influencers. Some of the board members may be connected with the groups in conflict. Other key influencers may have been a part of the historical review and understood the divine message to the church. If they have taken ownership of the process and agree with the implications, they can speak as a member of their conflicted group to help bring reconciliation.

I have ministered in a church that had an ongoing doctrinal conflict over Calvinism-Arminianism. This tore the church apart and kept it from being effective in the community. It took several board members sitting on opposite sides of the controversy to take ownership of the sinfulness of their attitudes toward one another. They agreed to disagree without being disagreeable any longer. They knew God was not commanding them to change their doctrinal position (as He would not command seniors necessarily to love contemporary Christian music, etc.). God *did* command them to love one another, and they had no excuse for the unloving things they had both said and done. As they confessed their unloving attitudes toward each other, they had a profound impact on all those involved in the controversy. It was like pouring a bucket of ice water on a hotspot. There was immediate relief.

Summary. Sinful reactivity is a common human problem connected with a tendency to increase the level of retaliation for a perceived injury. This can quickly spiral out of control. It is extremely common in evangelical churches where parishioners tend to spiritualize their conflicts and raise them to cosmic proportions—good vs. evil, God vs. the devil. They demonize the opposition and justify many of their sinful reactions and attitudes. All churches have such incidents, but if Christ is addressing your church in this area, the reactivity will have become serious and ministry-defeating over time.

These incidents often occur in hotspots, specific groups that continue to have and to hold conflict, perhaps over decades. To deal with repeated incidents of sinful reactivity, these hotspots need to be identified from the historical review. The fundamental counseling principle "what it's about is often not what it's about" needs to be applied to the situation because anger, once expressed, tends to dominate all emotional issues. There may have been a reason for the anger that needs to be addressed before the hotspot will cool down.

Genesis 4 indicates there is a "right thing to do" with anger and reactivity. One option for the church is a solemn assembly, a week of meetings (usually at the first of the year but it could occur anytime), which prepare people for repentance and reconciliation with each other and God. In these meetings, key leaders and influencers who understand the significance of the history and who represent the different groups that have been in conflict can speak on the group's behalf. They can confess the sins of the group and repent.

Chapter 13

LEADING THE CONGREGATION TO HEALING: PAST SHAME

In 1994, the leadership of the Southern Baptist denomination made a ground-breaking decision. They came to the conclusion that the history of their denomination was replete with shamefully racist attitudes and practices when it came to its relationship with African-Americans. The leaders acknowledged this had been true since the Southern Baptists split from the Northern Baptists over abolition prior to the Civil War. They stood in the place of all the pastors and church members of one hundred and forty years of their denomination and took responsibility for the sins of these individuals and churches. They wept in brokenness, confession and repentance before their gathered African-American brothers. They realized they couldn't undo a shameful past, but they needed to take responsibility for it and seek forgiveness in the present.

This morally courageous act of identificational repentance on the part of the mediatorial leadership of a whole denomination has had a profound, ongoing impact. Did every Southern Baptist church put away its collection of racist attitudes and practices the instant this happened? Of course not. But it did open the door to fundamental changes in the heart of the denomination, changes that continue to amaze onlookers. As I write this, a close African-American friend of mine has been called as the pastor of an *all-white* Southern Baptist congregation on the outskirts of Washington, D.C. I don't believe this could have happened ten years ago.

These leaders did, at the denominational level, the very things that need to be implemented at the church level.

ROOTING OUT PAST SHAME

During your historical review, you may come across stories of shameful incidents that occurred decades ago but still reside in the memory (and story-telling) of your church. In churches that are more than seventy-five years old, you may read about these incidents in the historical record of the church.

Jesus never stops speaking to your church about these things. Remember Matthew 23:30-32. Jesus quotes the attitude of the scribes of His own day who sought to separate themselves from responsibility for the shameful acts of their ancestors: *"'If we had lived in the days of our forefa-thers, we would not have taken part with them in shedding the blood of the prophets.' So you testify against yourselves that you are the descendants of those who murdered the prophets. Fill up, then, the measure of the sin of your forefathers!"* (NIV)

Churches and church leaders often operate under the same illusion as the scribes, thinking time heals all wounds or at least limits liability for them. Present enlightenment does not free a people from their past evils. The laws of the land may allow for a statute of limitations, but God does not! If your church is known for some shameful past action in the community, or carries in its collective memory some shameful event, God has not released the church from its responsibility regarding that event, though it may be a century old. The sons and daughters, whether the physical or spiritual offspring of those who perpetrated the actions, still "fill up their fathers' guilt" until they take responsibility for it.

Though it is difficult for believers today to accept this scriptural principle, the evidences of its truth abound in our society and in many of our churches. As a pastor, you must see and understand the significance of such a principle to your church. Such shameful actions and attitudes impact your church's heart. The church at Laodecia had a similar struggle seeing their spiritual condition. Jesus quotes them and then describes their actual shameful status in Revelation 3:17-18: *"You say, 'I am rich; I have acquired wealth and don't need a thing.' But you don't realize that you are wretched, pitiful, poor, blind and naked. I counsel you to buy from me gold refined in the fire, so you can become rich; and white clothes to wear, so you can cover your shameful nakedness; and salve to put on your eyes, so you can see"* (NIV).

Though the Laodecian church was "moneyed," yet at its heart there was a self-satisfied smugness that would have precipitated countless spiritual repercussions to a pastor and the church's ministry. Jesus tells them (and us) that He does not stop dealing with them because of the nature of his love: *"Those whom I love I rebuke and discipline. So be earnest, and repent"* (Rev. 3:19 NIV). The rebukes and discipline of Jesus are ongoing. They manifest themselves in the church's honest historical review.

It is similar to a family whose shame is hidden behind an "identified patient," a family member who becomes so "problemed" and sick that he absorbs all the family's attention so the family never has to deal with the real source of its pain. In churches, that individual is often the pastor.

If, after a historical review, you have not come across an explanation for why your church is inexplicably struggling, the answer may lay in hidden shame. The roots of your church's conflicts, its losses, its cliques, its controlling people may well have their origins in a corporate shame.

1. RACISM AND PREJUDICE

Racism is a loaded term. Many African-Americans believe that whites in America can never be the victims of racism because they hold most of the power. Racism, they would say, can only be perpetrated against minorities who are oppressed because of race and don't have access to the halls of power (even if the laws on the books indicate they do). My definition is broader when it comes to churches. Any church that—formally or informally—teaches, practices or holds attitudes that devalue people of another color or culture—people for whom Jesus died—is racist at heart. Such shame in the corporate heart requires cleansing.

Often such prejudice is automatic and ingrained. In Canada where I pastored for thirteen years, there was an almost universal prejudice against Americans, particularly white Americans (they tend not to see African- or Chinese-Americans as Americans). I remember expressing concern about this anti-American prejudice to a woman when I came to candidate. Her reply was a classic definition of "prejudice"—pre-judgment—based on stereotypes. "Oh," she replied in all sincerity, "It's true. I hate Americans . . . except for the ones I have met!"

Identifying racism in your church. In America, many churches have incidents involving race and racism in their collective memories, whether towards African-Americans or Hispanics or Asians. Some churches have histories of bailing out of a deteriorating neighborhood or failing to integrate while their neighborhoods changed color. Such churches will justify their actions by falling back on the "homogeneous principle." Though the originators of that theory of church growth never intended for what it became, churches and pastors use it to maintain segregation. Sociologists Michael Emerson and Christian Smith, in their book *Divided by Faith: Evangelical Religion and the Problem of Race in America*,[vii] substantiate that the failure to integrate and fellowship across cultural and racial lines maintains racist attitudes in white evangelical churches. Martin Luther King Jr. rightly observed,

"Sunday morning at 11:00 a.m. in America is the most segregated hour of the week."

Whites and blacks are not the only ones with issues like this between them, though by far they are the largest group. Slavery and Jim Crow attitudes still have not been fully resolved from the African-American point of view because white leaders have never taken full responsibility for them. White leaders have not yet said, "What do we have to do to make this right?" Racist issues also exist where Asians have set up businesses in ghettos and are resented, even hated, by African-Americans. In major cities, turf wars sometimes spill over from gangs to churches. Hispanics will have nothing to do with African-Americans who live on the next block, and an African-American would not dare to think of attending a Hispanic church service. How this must grieve God's heart!

Specific racist acts may be a part of your church's history. People of color may have been asked to leave or made to feel unwelcome in times past. Racist petitions may have circulated and segregationist meetings may have been held in the church. In a church where I consulted, they had a statement in the official minutes of the board from 1964 entitled "The Negro Problem." The statement said "All Negroes are welcome to hear the Word of God, but so as to cause no ill-feeling, they should not be invited to attend this church."

In white churches of the southern United States, these actions may have happened recently. In the western United States, the prejudices may have been against Native Americans or Chinese decades back. There may have been horrific acts of violence—lynchings, police shootings of innocent people, the KKK or gang violence—against people of color in your community while your church stood silently by. The Holy Spirit keeps alive the impact on the heart of the church through its storytelling and collective memory. Such shame and guilt in the corporate conscience begs to be cleansed. How do you do it?

Cleansing the shame. Agree as leaders to prepare your congregation for such a cleansing. It is important to seek out and begin to build personal relationships with pastors or community leaders from the racial or ethnic backgrounds representing the groups your church has offended. Discuss with them the offending items in your historical review and what God has said to your leaders and your church about them. You must not withhold the effects on the church of failing to listen to God for decades. Don't be surprised if these pastors weep as you share the story. They carry the wound deep in their hearts, too.

With the help of caring leaders from both churches, *together* design a service of racial reconciliation *filled with symbols and symbolic actions*. You both need to be sensitive to each other's culture and ethnic uniqueness. In the months prior to this event, nothing will be more important in your congregation. Prayer, sensitivity and care should undergird this event. When the time comes, the congregation should know exactly what they are doing and exactly why they are doing it.

If you are in a predominately white church seeking to reconcile with the black church or the black community, exercise particular sensitivity. Let the pastor of a black church educate you on the way African-Americans interpret even well-meaning efforts of whites. Inviting them to your church may not be the wisest thing. It could smack of "being told to come up to the big house" reminiscent of slave times. Also many blacks are quite cynical about "white folk" who have pretty words but then don't do anything to stand up, speak out, or get active for racial equality. Part of your church's commitment must go beyond exchanging pulpits once a year or having choirs sing in each other's churches.

If your church carries guilt for racial events in the past, restitution needs to be part of your response. In 2 Samuel 21, David asked the Gibeonites Saul abused and persecuted, "How can I make amends so that you will bless the Lord's inheritance?"(21:3) This needs to be honestly asked of those who have been hurt by racism. The Gibeonites first response was, "We don't want anything." However, David (and God) was not satisfied with that response. Nor should you be. Find appropriate ways to express your repentance long-term. Setting up a scholarship fund for black young people from a certain church to attend a Bible college or seminary can communicate the right things. Offering to involve your people in some of their ministries in an appropriate fashion also may be significant. Do something other than just "pretty words."

Reading books such as David Anderson and Brent Zuercher's Letters *Across the Divide: Two Friends Explore Racism, Friendship and Faith* (Baker, 2001), Glen Kehrein and Raleigh Washington's *Breaking Down Walls* (Moody, 1993), and Tony Evans' *Let's Get to Know Each Other* (Thomas Nelson, 1995) are great ways to increase racial understanding and sensitivity. For deeper study, read the before-mentioned *Divided by Faith* by Emerson and Smith.

Will everyone agree with your course of action? Probably not. Expect resistance. But take heart! Remember Moses at Kadesh Barnea (Numbers 14). Even God's clear leadership and direction could not convince a people frightened by the obstacles or limited by their prejudices. However, it is a sign of good spiritual leadership to try.

2. SOCIOECONOMIC SNOBBERY

The part of the city where our church was located was the object of some prejudice in Toronto. I remember one well-heeled couple from a wealthy neighborhood (not our part of the city) that started attending. Their daughter became quite involved in our youth group. However, they left our church as soon as she began to be interested in one of the boys (to quote them) "from *that* side of town."

Identifying snobbery in your church. Churches in communities are often divided into haves and have-nots. As with racism, your church may hold or have held an attitude of devaluation toward a certain *class* of people who are of the same color and culture as the majority of your people. This can be subtle and difficult to detect in the church's history.

Many churches today try to protect their children from the influences of "neighborhood kids" and their churches from "neighborhood people." They set up a class system in their Sunday schools and youth ministries to keep their "good Christian kids" away from the neighborhood "riff-raff" or "troublemakers." One realizes the spiritual seriousness of this attitude by asking, "If Jesus were on earth, to which group would He most likely be found ministering?"

A church with which I consulted once employed a youth pastor who had a dynamic outreach to street people. Literally dozens of these individuals—prostitutes, drug addicts, the homeless—started attending the church. The youth pastor would gather them in on Sunday morning and they all sat together in the front four pews! They were not beyond high-fiving each other when the pastor made a good point. One time a leather-clad individual leaned over to another and said loudly, "S***! That is awesome!" Unfortunately, the church leadership marshaled the homogeneous principle to justify trying to stifle the youth pastor or focus his ministry on "our kind of person." When he refused to be stifled, they fired him. That is a shame in more ways than one!

How would your church respond to such an influx of "that kind of person?" How has it responded? Picture them: unwashed, unkempt, scantily clad, sporting mohawks, tattoos, and body piercings galore—all front and center in your church. This becomes a true test of a church's heart for evangelism and measures it against God's value system. These people matter to God. Did your church have a heart big enough, mature enough to see beyond the outward dress to the inward need? If not, that story would be in your church's history, kept alive by the Spirit, requiring repentance.

Jesus says, "And you don't realize that *you* (sing.) are wretched, pitiful, poor, blind and naked. . . . Those whom I love I rebuke and discipline. So be earnest, and repent" (Revelation 3:17,19 NASV). Mother Teresa said something similar when someone stuck a microphone in her face as she exited from a limousine to receive an award. "How do you feel about all this wealth around you?" the reporter asked.

"There are more kinds of poverty than just one," she replied.

Snobbery filters into all ministries until the "wealthy" (whether the monetarily or spiritually advantaged) get favored treatment. This is not a new problem to the church. James describes a very similar circumstance occurring in the early church in James 2:1-7.

> My brothers, as believers in our glorious Lord Jesus Christ, don't show favoritism. Suppose a man comes into your meeting wearing a gold ring and fine clothes, and a poor man in shabby clothes also comes in. If you show special attention to the man wearing fine clothes and say, "Here's a good seat for you," but say to the poor man, "You stand there" or "Sit on the floor by my feet," have you not discriminated among yourselves and become judges with evil thoughts? Listen, my dear brothers: Has not God chosen those who are poor in the eyes of the world to be rich in faith and to inherit the kingdom he promised those who love him? But you have insulted the poor. Is it not the rich who are exploiting you? Are they not the ones who are dragging you into court? Are they not the ones who are slandering the noble name of him to whom you belong? (NIV)

Discrimination has many forms, some of which are quite subtle but all of which are shameful for a corporate gathering of believers.

Cleansing the shame. As church leaders and mediatorial authorities you should lead your congregation in repentance for these attitudes. You should pay whatever the price to purchase the "white garments" Jesus recommends to the church at Laodecia, so that "the shame of your nakedness may not be revealed." Socioeconomic snobbery is not easy to identify, so knowing how to cleanse it becomes more difficult.

Here's a suggestion: Find a church from a "side of town" (but not far away) that your congregation has looked down upon, build a relationship with the pastor, and ultimately his church might pave the way for a joint service of repentance and reconciliation. Chances are they will have felt snubbed in times past. Many churches carry a reputation for such attitudes, and in an honest moment the pastor might admit that people in his church have felt this way about your church.

Your church should be primed for this joint service and understand what they are doing and why. Prepare them by preaching a series on James or on

God's view of the "monetarily challenged." (You know I'm kidding, right?) There are some powerful passages about God's view of the poor. Explain what you are going to do at the joint service and why repentance is necessary. Invite your congregation to remember when they have felt the sting of devaluation for some characteristic or condition about which they could do little. Illustrate this any way you can—with drama or interview or testimony— to help people feel how wrong it is to devalue people based on outward conditions. Invite them to join in the repentance of the leadership at the joint service.

Curiosity will cause many that don't otherwise understand to show up. However, if you sense the spirit of your church is responsive, an open microphone to hear such repentance from individual congregation members could be an amazing addition to the service. Members of the other church might respond with confession of bad attitudes and envy. Prayerfully prepared for, such a service can heal many wounds in the hearts of both churches. God will confirm your obedience through supernatural blessings.

The connection between churches needs to be ongoing. Pulpit exchanges and joint services on Good Friday might become a way of solidifying your relationship with the cross-town church. Joint ministry efforts further strengthen the bond. Ask God to show you specific ways to do it. Go beyond just pretty words.

3. ETHICAL PROBLEMS

The many faces of ethical shame. There have always been people who use the local church for less than honorable purposes. These unethical people and their practices make the news all the time. Many churches have become scam headquarters for lining the pockets or enlarging of the fiefdoms of nefarious individuals. Some have convinced lay leaders to "bend the rules" of the church constitution. If your church has such a person, persons, or events in its past, they may come up in the historical review. The Spirit keeps the memory alive until someone takes responsibility for it and deals with it by means of public confession and cleansing.

Bottom line: A failure in ethics creates a distrust of leadership. The more incidents of unethical behavior you uncover in the storytelling of your church's past, the more corporate distrust of the leadership grows, even if the present leadership is trustworthy. You will sense manifestations of this distrust both atmospherically (whenever the leadership speaks) and see it in the response to leadership initiatives and decision-making, particularly in the areas where the breech occurred. Again, this will happen, even if the breech was a decade or more before. The wound is still in the heart of the church.

Churches have had boards or pastors who have ignored the covenant that exists between the leadership and the congregation in the form of the church constitution and bylaws. Like legal shysters, they have looked for loopholes in order to achieve their own purposes. I confess to having faced that temptation a number of times as I felt strapped by a constitution that prevented me from accomplishing some ministry goal. True, such documents should be our servants rather than our masters, but we create ethical problems if we violate them without following due process. They are a statement of promise to a congregation that the leaders will follow certain guidelines. To renege knowingly on a promise has the same effect corporately as it does individually. As our culture has seen a decline in the level of commitment to covenants, church leaders have not escaped this manifestation of unfaithfulness. When a congregation catches its leaders in a deliberate act of subterfuge, it creates a wound of distrust that needs healing. The congregation keeps the incident (and issue) alive in its heart by storytelling.

Money is the root of all sorts of shame in churches because of the evil that it can cause. The necessity of fundraising and fundraising techniques forms a weed-bed of ethical problems. The end comes to justify the less-than-spiritual means of raising money. Pastors and boards have lost their faith and integrity over the pressure of a multi-million dollar mortgage or the crushing demands of raising money to pay the bills each month. Many an architect's dream for a church building has killed a pastor's ministry through burnout or compromised a pastor's integrity through pressure to raise the money for it by any means possible.

The pressure can be unbearable and the results devastating. One pastor friend told me that he had to raise $15,000 a month from his church just to *pay the interest* on the loan for their new building. "We might as well burn that money on the front steps," he said. "It does not purchase anything—just the right to have the loan." Another pastor told me how his new building turned people into dollar signs. "New people entered our church, and all I could see in them was help for our debt." One church had a million dollar missions budget and kept raising money for missions with elaborate conferences, but didn't pay their missionaries for two years since the leadership instead channeled the money into a building project. When these circumstances came out, it damaged the image of the church and its ministry, creating a monumental wound of distrust. This story has a happy ending though, through courageous repentance and restitution.

Many churches have an incident in their history where someone in spiritual leadership has absconded with church funds. An elder, a deacon, a trustee, or a pastor may have embezzled or stolen church offerings. A pastor may have been caught overcharging an expense account or felt "justified" in using church funds to make personal purchases. Often boards will attempt to keep this information "among the leadership." Seldom does it stay there. However, even though the culprit may have been brought to justice, a wound of distrust remains in the heart of the church.

Healing ethical shame. Bringing healing to the heart of a church that has experienced a shameful breech of ethics is easier in that it remains "in house." If there are events involving a previous pastor or previous boards, I have already described the ability and responsibility present leadership has as the church's mediatorial authorities to stand in the place of those that have gone before and take responsibility for their sins. The wounds caused by the sins of others have inflicted the church's heart. The present leadership deals with these past sins through identificational repentance.

Plan for a service of repentance by the leadership. The pastor should prime the congregation with a series of messages on godly leadership or the impact of ungodly leadership. Preaching on selected kings of Israel and Judah could set the stage, or perhaps focusing on King David, whose life shows both the benefits of godly leadership and the devastating effects of unethical choices on the part of leadership. Build up to the service by telling some of the stories you learned in the historical review. I can guarantee some members, even among your leaders, won't like the pastor "airing the church's dirty laundry." There are powerful forces working to keep such information under wraps. My response has always been: "I agree we need to bury this stuff, but we need to give it a *Christian burial*." God gives us only one way to do that—repentance and cleansing.

You can call your service a reconciliation service or leadership Sunday or even a recommissioning service of leadership. Prepare the church by telling them what you are doing and why. Tie your explanation into the sermons that have been preached. Get the congregation curious. During that service, the pastor and members of the boards should take responsibility for the specific unethical acts through identification with the perpetrators.

The declaration of repentance sounds something like this (adapt it to your own situation):

Today we stand in the place of those who wounded this church through shameful behavior. We have felt the power of the temptations they faced. We know in our hearts that we are no different from them. We come before you today in their place to take responsibility for the way they [violated the church constitution, used unethical means to raise money, took the Lord's money you gave to the church and used it in inappropriate ways]. We ask you and the Lord to forgive us for this sinful violation of the most important thing we have between us—trust! And we seek to be recommissioned before the Lord and you today, a fresh clean start for us as your God-appointed leaders.

The church I mentioned earlier, that used several million dollars of designated mission funds for building purposes and didn't pay their missionaries for two years, replaced its pastor. When the new pastor found out what had happened, he performed a magnificent service of identificational repentance. He called in the heads of all the mission boards and agencies for a service, and as many missionaries as were available. On the platform in a Sunday service he repented and asked forgiveness before them all. He pledged that the church would make up for the shortfall. The courageous leadership of a pastor who understood the power of identificational repentance turned what could have spelled long-term disaster for this church into a marvelous healing of the church's heart. It works.

4. MORAL SHAME

Has your church ever had its name in the newspaper other than in an advertisement? More and more churches find themselves the subject of investigation for sexual abuse and pedophilia. The media splashes the name of the church over the front page and assumes guilt before a trial ever occurs. Whether the charges end up being true or not, the publicity creates a wound of shame kept alive in the memory of the church.

If the charges are true, the wound is grave and cries for healing. The higher the position, responsibility and visibility of the perpetrator, the more devastating the corporate wound. As with an individual experiencing abuse, these wounds don't heal easily or quickly. The congregation parallels the typical family dynamics with abuse: they are the wounds people in the congregation will most want to cover and never discuss. Victims or their parents may still attend the church and people will fear "stirring up" the old pain. Yet the reality is that this hasn't happened without God's knowledge. Might this devastating corporate pain and shame be God's megaphone summoning the church to something unique? What would Jesus say to a church with this kind of wound in its past? How would He want them to deal with it?

Events may have occurred over a decade or more before the present pastor got there. He probably didn't hear about it when candidating, but it would come out in the historical review. The leadership needs to stop and examine that event for a while even if it is the last thing they want to do. It is critical for them to sense what God was saying to the church through its pain at that time, what it needed to learn and may still need to learn.

The present leaders need to process how the leadership of that time responded, how they handled communication, the community reaction, the victims and their families, and finally the perpetrator. You don't do this to blame the previous leadership but to assess where the present leaders need to take responsibility in identificational repentance. They need to analyze the way the congregation reacted and if the trauma created a corporate "way of pain," a pattern of behavior that continues to poison the atmosphere of the church.

Healing moral shame. No church will be happy or feel healthy after events like this, nor should it. Did God, like Elijah's taunt of Baal, "go on vacation" when this happened? Do we believe in Christ's power to heal? Is it possible He has a positive purpose for the devastation? Can He bring "beauty from ashes?"

You should ask as you do your historical review: "We know He tests us to see what is in our heart—what did these tragedies show us about our church?" Do you believe the manifestation of His reality in this sin-cursed world comes through His power to comfort and heal when all the doctors say healing is impossible? His agenda for the church expands to include what will be done with the comfort received (see 2 Cor.1:3-5). If the church leaders don't grasp these things, who else will?

Let me speak to the advisability of a service for a trauma like this. Only in the rarest of occasions could you hold a public service where you rehearse the details of the trauma. The victims are the most important people in a situation like this, and you have a moral obligation not to victimize them further. On a rare occasion, victims may want to extend public forgiveness to a perpetrator, and a service on that theme could be enormously powerful to heal the heart of your church from its wound.

That does not mean we have no other way to give something like this a Christian burial. Sadly, as in the heart of the abuse victim, it cannot be forever erased from the memory of the church, a painful reminder of the horror of sin. Actually it helps the victim to acknowledge this ever-present corporate pain and sorrow. Abuse victims are like war veterans in many ways. They want to forget the horrors of war, but they want everyone else to remember the war so that they honor the survivors, recall the emotional and physical scars they bear, and work diligently never to let war happen again. It is important to war veterans to have a Memorial Day or a Remembrance Day where once a year their pain of loss, and the country's loss, is remembered.

I wonder if this was not part of God's purpose behind Yom Kippur. The Israelites had their daily sacrifices for sin, but once a year the whole country came together to remember the sin of the corporate body. The High Priest as the mediatorial authority offered a sacrifice for everyone together. The impact of sin on the corporate body is something we are not sensitive to in our Western culture.

The Apostle Paul wanted the whole Corinthian congregation to feel the impact and sense the corporate danger of the sin of the man cohabiting with his stepmother. He told them they should mourn and recognize that failing to act was letting poison (leaven) loose in their corporate body. As stated in chapter 3, I believe it was the responsibility of the mediatorial authorities of the congregation to lead them in the proper response to the corporate effects of the sin. If this response was true for the son and stepmother who willingly chose to violate God's commands, how much more corporate mourning should there be when a predator has been loose in your church?

I also wonder if something similar to Yom Kippur could not be built into a church calendar when a sexual predator has traumatized the church, a day or service of corporate mourning for all those who have been victims of the sin of others. Such a general presentation would not single out victims of the perpetrator alone, but open the door for a healing for all who have experienced such pain. No church ministry can sustain itself weekly dwelling on such pain, but yearly there could be a time of "remembrance" so as to honor the survivors, recall the scars of body and spirit they bear, and commit corporately to work to prevent such devastation from happening again. This would go a long way to healing the heart of your church.

When the perpetrator's family is present. A word about one of the more difficult circumstances God will use to test a church's heart—when the perpetrator of a crime has his or her family present in the church. Most will leave a church in embarrassment when sordid revelations are uncovered about a family member. They will find some place where they are not known and make a fresh start. However, on occasion some don't. It is critical to recognize that they are victims too.

An incident in a church nearby brings this point home. A young mother asked another older woman in her congregation to watch her infant on an ongoing basis. This woman generally watched children ages four and up, so at first she refused. The young mom was desperate and begged, and finally the older woman agreed. While in this baby-sitter's care, the unthinkable happened—the infant died. An autopsy showed the baby had been shaken severely and police charged the baby-sitter with murder. The story was plastered on the front pages of all the newspapers.

Meanwhile both families stayed in the church. The pastor, in an effort to handle honestly the sad tension now existing in his congregation, preached a message on compassion to the hurting, and applied it to the needs of both the victim's families, and to the families of the perpetrators. His message split the church and made the newspapers again. Some were so angry and offended at the perpetrator that, as so often happens, guilt-by-association made them want to blame everyone in the family too. There was no question in their minds that this woman was a *murderer*. No compassion should be shown to her *or* her kin, not while the victim's family sat right there!

This huge illustration can serve for all lesser ones. This pastor faced an unenviable situation of having people related to victim and perpetrator sitting in front of him. Some of you may face a similar dilemma. In healing the heart of your church, some of the people who participated in sinful activity and those wounded by it will also be present as you seek to resolve the past sinfulness. Remember that you are a body, and that God empowers mediatorial authorities to act on behalf of the corporate body for which they are responsible. However, they can not, they *must* not separate themselves into "us" vs. "them." They have to own what has happened as *their own*. This was the way of all the mediatorial authorities the Bible presents—whether kings or priests. When they confessed the sin of their people, they confessed it as their own, either personally or collectively. (See 2 Chron. 6; Ez. 9:6-7; Neh. 1:5-11; Ps. 106:6; Jer. 3:25; Dan. 9, etc.) The pastor and church leaders stand for the body. If the sin happened within their congregation, it belongs to them, and if wounds have occurred because of the sin, they own those too. That mentality gives them a huge clue as to how to handle it publicly.

Another important aspect is balance. It wasn't that what the pastor said in the above illustration was not true or his goal was not right, he just needed to *give recognition to both sides as he needed to take ownership of the crime*. His congregation on the other hand *rightly* represented and symbolized the tension that existed in the heart of God over the murder of that child. True guilt exists and it demands justice. However, there is also the willingness on God's part to forgive when one takes ownership of the guilt and there is repentance from the heart, no matter what the sin. Both are absolutely true.

Pastors often want to rush to resolve the tension, thinking that tension is a terrible thing. *Tension like this is absolutely normal.* Indeed, *God feels this tension* in His great heart *all the time*, the tension of Law versus Grace, of Justice versus Mercy. *How appropriate that God should invite His children into the experience of the tension!*

A common mistake in counseling is failing to validate a victim's hurt and anger before trying to lead him or her to forgive the perpetrator. Such a failure in balance results in an inadequate and incomplete forgiveness. The weight of forgiveness is measured by the weight of the crime (Jesus taught there were "weightier matters" of law in Matthew 23:20). If you fail to validate the anger and pain, and instead hurry to forgiveness or compassion, you will inflame the anger and create resistance instead.

Forgiveness acts as a powerful antidote to an abuse victim's pain. One does not extend forgiveness for the sake of the perpetrator—only God ultimately can forgive a perpetrator. Forgiveness at the human level frees the one forgiving from holding onto pain and anger that can be life-limiting and destructive. God teaches us to forgive for *our* sake, not the perpetrator's sake.

Church leaders need to remember this as they work to heal the corporate heart, especially when they are dealing with people who have been seriously hurt in their congregation. If any of the victims (or their families) sense the diminishment or devaluation of their pain or lessening of the seriousness of the crime by rushing to forgiveness, they will react. Therefore church leaders need to open their hearts fully to the experience both of the victim and the perpetrator—the perpetrator because we are all sinners, and the victim because we are all victims of the sins of others. I believe that is why the apostle Paul counseled corporate mourning in 1 Corinthians 5 and Jesus regularly instructed the churches in Revelation 2 and 3 to repent corporately. Repentance, to be honest and effective, takes ownership of the seriousness of the sin. Once the repentance is made wholeheartedly, forgiveness has a chance of being extended individually and corporately. Because God allows people to choose it freely or not, there are no sure-fire guarantees, but at least the possibility exists.

"Wait a second," I hear some of you saying. "How can the pastor or church leaders honestly repenting help the families of victims and perpetrators?" You've discovered the crux of the book! *No pain affecting members of the congregation because they are members of the congregation is ever anything less than corporate.* The bigger the issue, the greater the wound, the more significant the impact on the church's heart. A wound unhealed continues to impact a church, sometimes for decades. Mediating authorities can embrace the pain on both sides and should. It is their God-given job! No one else can do it! They must own it in order to lead people corporately to the One who can heal it.

The pastor who has the families of both victims and perpetrators sitting in front of him can pray something like this:

Our Father, we cannot raise our heads to you because of the sorrow and shame that fills our hearts. Our church has become a place where pain of the worst kind has been inflicted on innocents. How this unspeakably grieves Your great heart. You watched Your Only Begotten Son abused and mistreated and killed by people who didn't understand the value of His life and you understand the pain of the family that has lost so much. We together as a church embrace that pain today with them. We would not leave them alone in it, even as You don't.

But, our Father, we know our hearts. We have sinned before you—all of us! We know that we daily hurt others, sometimes in ignorance, but often knowingly. Your word indicates that if we become angry with our brother, we are murderers at heart, for anger is the fountainhead of murder. Who then among us is not a murderer today? Who should escape Your justice? Who could cast the first stone if that is Your divine measurement? How do you tolerate us knowing the way we are? How is it that we are not consumed?

Yet You do so much more than tolerate us. How we stand amazed at Your justice; but we stand even more amazed at Your grace, that you can embrace sinful people like us and love us enough to send Your Son as a sacrifice, to bear our sin, which today we feel is great beyond our comprehension, and to forgive us.

Who can heal this wound in our heart, but You? We unite our hearts here today to seek that healing and the process by which it will come fully. We together, from our hearts, declare Your right-eousness this day and look forward to the Day coming when all things will be made right. Thank You for Your mercy and grace that can sustain us until that time.

Some will challenge such teaching—exaggerating the point to reject it. They might retort: "That means you would be holding a repentance service every Sunday! There is always sinful, shameful activity going on in a church—gossip, hypocrisy, lust, and envy. When would repentance stop?" You certainly should be mindful of the destructive power of sin to keep you dependent on Christ and His grace as you meet week by week. If church leadership deals with the big things, they will have a better sense of what to do with the lesser things. That is not a dodge. The things that God has been speaking to a church about must be addressed by the church. Corporate obedience can have an enormous impact. The blessing of God becomes extremely motivating.

Summary: A church can experience a number of things that produce corporate guilt and shame. 1) There are many geographical areas where racism or cultural prejudices have been an issue in churches. People in a congregation keep shameful stories alive in the church's memory and retell them regularly. 2) Socio-economic snobbery, a form of class prejudice, may have had an impact on your church's heart. 3) Ethical failures over fund-raising, stolen money, or broken covenants sometime in the past may have created a climate of distrust in church leadership. 4) Moral failure in its many forms may have stained the heart of your church.

The ways of addressing these shameful events differ in type, but not in purpose. When possible, you should invite the people who have been hurt or their representatives to a service where repentance is made and forgiveness is sought. In the case of abuse victims, be careful not to cause further injury, so more private works of repentance are done.

In that rare instance where you have victims, perpetrators, and/or their families sitting in front of you, you can still address the wound by fully identifying with both victim and perpetrator in your repentance before God. Church leaders should resist the desire to relieve tension by rushing to forgiveness without fully validating the injuries.

Chapter 14

WRITING THE NEXT CHAPTER OF YOUR HISTORY

We've finally reached the fun part! No more having to read the want ads with longing or the obituaries with envy. Thank God!

First, let's review the process. Your church leaders have labored to do the hard work of corporate spiritual physicians. Together you have learned much about yourselves and your church that you never realized before. Everyone has come to see the depth of connection that exists over the generations of believers who may have sat in the church's pews and of the corporate heart that held the wounds and shame of past days. Jesus, in His love and wisdom, had kept communicating to your church about the need to face these things. He emphasized the need to cleanse her heart through permitting a series of painful events, often repeated in a cyclic pattern, usually with pastor after pastor. "Those whom I love, I rebuke and discipline," He kept saying to you all, "so be earnest and repent" (Rev. 3:19). Now you have listened and heard Him, obeyed and responded to Him.

The rebuke and discipline of Jesus is not fun, but His objective is clear. The present church leadership owns the sins of the past and knows it must deal with them. Christ uniquely equips the church leadership to do so by delegating to them His mediating authority. They can stand in the place of those under their authority or those past people in their leadership roles who may have sinned and speak for them. They initiate a service to perform identificational repentance before God and those in the congregation who have been injured, effectively cleansing the church's heart.

In that service as the leaders address and cleanse the painful events of the past, they invite people to bring their own wounds to Christ for healing and to forgive those who may have injured them. They create symbols and establish them for remembrance. Be prepared to experience the corporate fruits of doing this good work—Jesus will start to bless your congregation in ways you could not have planned or imagined.

The energy drain stops. The first thing that happens is a restoration of corporate spiritual and emotional health. The church has finally listened to and obeyed its Lord! At the beginning of the book, I said that the reason leaders should go through this long process is to be able to free their church from things that bind it and prevent it from becoming all God wants it to be. Once the church's heart has been healed, the church's reservoir of spiritual power becomes available to accomplish ministry that had not been there previously.

Why is that? Just like the physical body, when the corporate body is sick, its energy becomes focused on healing and there is not much energy available for external ministry. Churches that are sick for a long time become extremely in-focused and strongly resistant to outreach initiatives. There are so many internal problems and pain, no one can think about ministry outside.

A new pastor may come in with a lot of energy and enthusiasm, and he may supply a "shot in the arm" by adding his energy to the mix. Churches that have "revolving-door pastors" (one after another) are living on this short-lived shot. Ultimately this type of pastor finds that he is *carrying* the church with his energy and burning himself out. His enthusiasm might have been "contagious" at first. The church may even grow significantly, but soon the sick, untreated state of the church restores corporate lethargy or raises old-time conflicts. Instead of him infecting the church with health, the church begins to infect him with its sickness. His energy sags as frustrations mount and burnout looms.

Healing the heart of your church changes all of that in a number of ways.

Use the new energy available. When the church's heart is healed, all that energy that had been focused on dealing with and defending its wounds now becomes available for ministry once again. God releases the power of the Holy Spirit as the Body finally responds in corporate obedience to the messages He has sent through the years. This energy gets translated into joy and a positive spirit that actually can be tangible to new people who enter the building. After we had our reconciliation service, our church experienced over two years of continual renewal, daily supernatural events within the congregation that manifested God's pleasure and presence in our midst.

Though you will want to revel and glory in the energy of the healthy corporate body (an appropriate response), giving leadership direction to the ministry now becomes more important than ever. That energy needs a ministry focus and a new vision for the future.

Seek God for a new ministry focus and a vision for the future.

It is also appropriate to once again organize a leadership retreat with the purpose of asking God where He wants you to go from here. As leaders, you can (and should) invite the congregation to pray for you as you go with this specific objective of listening to God for what is next for your church. What does He want you to do now?

Your historical review of the church helps in another significant way at this point. The leaders should have a sense of the flow of the church's history and the major lessons God has taught it. Some of these lessons involved pain, but some of them came in the form of blessings upon ministry efforts. There is a reason why God has your church where it is.

There is wisdom in connecting any new vision to the original vision the founders had for the church when they started it. Your development of a new vision can flow from your church's original purpose and the ministries God blessed through the years. There are a number of reasons for finding a way to connect a new vision for the church's future with its history.

First, the *old-timers and church founders*, many of whom are probably still the core of the church, will appreciate it. If the leadership works to tie the original vision to the new vision, you gain their support and encouragement. It will affirm that what they believed and worked for decades ago had value. Many older members feel that the new generation cares nothing for the old and does not believe they know how to worship or evangelize. We often send that message as pastors when we talk about doing something new. To root the new vision in the values and purpose of the original church affirms the ministry of those who labored through those years and gains their support.

Second, and similarly, connecting the visions demonstrates *appropriate* respect for the past. I would be surprised if one in ten pastors who moves into an existing ministry takes time to get to know the history of the church. Such an assignment is generally not on their "to-do" list. They have their agendas and begin to work them out. When pastors cast a new vision for their churches, they often unwittingly denigrate the history and tradition within a church. To justify a new vision we often dismiss the old ways of doing things. Why else make a change? Jesus warned of the impact of trying to pour new wine into old wineskins. Rooting the new vision in the past can prevent such a rupture.

You may need to retranslate that original vision into contemporary language for your modern church culture and community. In addition, you and the church will have learned some significant things about corporate pain and how to heal it. God has given you another whole set of skills and experiences that other churches desperately need. Doubtless God will draw upon those resources for the sake of others. Don't ignore this. God comforts us so we can give the comfort away, whether individually or corporately (see 2 Cor. 1:3-5).

Go to the seminars, read the books! Now your church leaders can begin to read books on church growth and go to seminars on vision-casting and realize that the possibility exists of implementing such ideas. I still believe pastors and church leaders need sensitivity to their own contexts and not try to mimic anyone else (for not every vision works for every church). The church and its leaders should now be listening to what God is saying to the corporate body. They can pray and listen to Him for direction about where to go from where the church is. That direction may well come from the timely input they receive in a book, seminar or conference.

Even if you decide to set off in a brand new direction and cast a new vision, your education in the church's history will enable you to "speak the language of the past" to connect the past with the future. Like Moses delivering the message of Deuteronomy, your future will be rooted in the lessons of the past. You will have the sensitivity to the values and culture of the church that will enable you to know how best to present such a vision for the future. With wisdom, the leadership can provide a sense of continuity and flow, of balance and of wholeness, and a sense of oneness of mind and heart as you move toward it. You may still face the normal obstacles that occur in implementing such changes, but they will be obstacles the books often describe, not the dysfunctional, destructive, draining roadblocks encountered previously.

Create a climate for listening to God. You never want your church to be in a position of failing to listen to God ever again. Jesus will continue to speak to your church as in Revelation 2 and 3, but the message may change depending on what the church does or fails to do. The leadership needs to create a climate for listening to what Jesus is saying to the church, both at the leadership level and the congregational level.

There may be more times of corporate pain and crises ahead for your church. God continues to test us to see what is in our hearts. The devil will still mount assaults, especially if your church becomes effective in reaching others and discipling them. Nothing you have done prevents these attacks and God will still speak through them. During such times you need to face each other at board meetings and ask, "Is the Lord trying to tell us something?" How much better to face such crises with a healthy church body rather than an unhealthy one! Take the lessons learned through the process of healing your church's heart and discern what God is saying through the pain.

Conclusion. If you have finished the process of healing the heart of your church, you are ready to write the new chapter, the future chapter, with hope. Your church is still a human family, and as such is far from perfect. It will still sin, still make mistakes. So will you as church leaders. There may be troubles to come. Nevertheless, you have learned a process that holds the hope for both finding out what God is saying at any time and taking steps that can put your church back in the place where God can use it to accomplish His purposes in the place where He has you. May God bless and guide you as you do.

> He who has an ear, let him hear what the Spirit says to the churches. To him who overcomes, I will give the right to eat from the tree of life, which is in the paradise of God (Rev. 2:7 NASV).

<u>APPENDIX</u>

The following is a format to use as a follow-up to the historical review of your church. Have the people who went on the retreat write a letter from Jesus to your church, incorporating the things learned in the review.

The Letter of Jesus to the Eighth Local Church – Ours!

Jesus wrote the seven letters of Revelation 2 and 3 to seven local churches with a variety of issues on His heart. He still speaks to local churches and has messages for them based on His Word. Assess what Jesus might be saying to your church. Write a letter in the format of the letters to the seven churches that you think Jesus might send to your local church.

Salutation: Some characterization of Jesus, attributes which might be apropos to your church.

Example: *"To the angel of the church in Ephesus write: 'The One who holds the seven stars in His right hand, the One who walks among the seven golden lampstands, says this:'" (Rev. 2:1 NASV)*

Clear Commendation: Jesus usually finds things to commend in the church. What would He commend in your church?

Example: *'I know your deeds and your toil and perseverance, and that you cannot endure evil men, and you put to the test those who call themselves apostles, and they are not, and you found them to be false; and you have perseverance and have endured for My name's sake, and have not grown weary. . . 'Yet this you do have, that you hate the deeds of the Nicolaitans, which I also hate' (Rev. 2:2-3,6).*

Constructive Criticism: Jesus puts His finger on some key issues at present and historically in the church. What would He point out as needing to be addressed in your local church?

Example: *'But I have this against you, that you have left your first love' (Rev. 2:4).*

Crucial Counsel: There is something your church needs to do to get right with Him again.

Example: *'Remember therefore from where you have fallen, and repent and do the deeds you did at first; or else I am coming to you, and will remove your lampstand out of its place—unless you repent' (Rev. 2:5).*

Promise to the Courageous: Those who do what Jesus says in the advice portion will "overcome" the obstacles to their growth and are promised some amazing things. What would He promise your people if they are courageous to do what He says?

Example: *'He who has an ear, let him hear what the Spirit says to the churches. To him who overcomes, I will grant to eat of the tree of life, which is in the Paradise of God' (Rev. 2:7).*

MODELS OF GENOGRAMS

A genogram is a "family map" which records vital relational information in a pictorial way. By its lines and connections, one can "see" the nature and impact of multigenerational patterns of behaviors which might not otherwise be recognized. The significance of genograms can be seen by mapping the family of Jacob according to Scriptural information.

The basic symbols for drawing a family map are below:

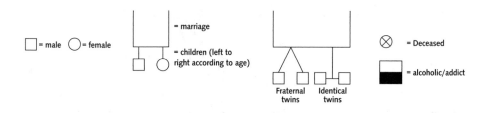

First, here is a simple genogram of one generation – Abram and Sarai – at the time of Abram's call to leave Ur.

Another important use of genograms is to show the nature of the relationships–closeness, distance, conflict, stress, cut-offs, fusion, separation and divorce. These are pictorially represented as follows:

Close	═══════
Very Close/P???	═══════
Distant	··············
Conflicted/Stressed	ᴠᴠᴠᴠᴠᴠ
Conflicted and Fused	⩘⩙⩘⩙⩘
Repressed??	─────╱───
Divorced	─────╫────
Cut Off	─────╱╱────

Here is a picture of Abraham's relationships with Sarah and Hagar with their children at the time of the conflict with Hagar and Ishmael over Isaac (Genesis 21). The ages of the individuals at that particular time are placed inside the symbols.

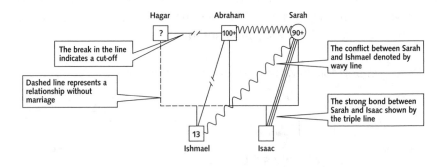

The next generation is also interesting as we focus on the "child of promise" – Isaac, Joseph's grandfather. Genograms can show more than the two generations. They can be linked to show multiple generations, such as at the birth of Jacob and Esau to Isaac and Rebecca.

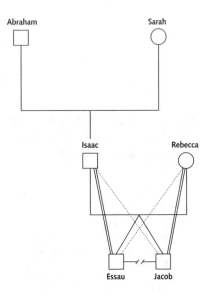

Remember the basic "legend" of the family map. This map shows the *three generations*, the sex (squares = males, circles = females), the *husband/wife relationship*, and the *children produced* and *their birth order*. In this case, because Esau and Jacob were fraternal twins, they branch off the same line (showing they were born at the same time). And we know something about how these relationships worked out. Isaac favored Esau and Rebecca favored Jacob. This ultimately resulted in the deception of Jacob when he stole Isaac's blessing, which produced his cut off from Esau for several decades.

Even complicated family maps can be drawn. Many people come from large families. Here is the map of Jacob and his wives and children with some of the family dynamics.

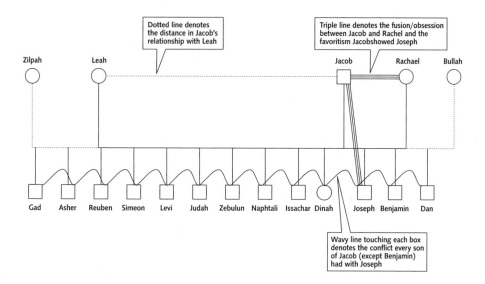

Using the space below (or a separate sheet of paper), draw your genogram for four generations (your grandparents, your parents, you and your wife, and your children). Using the legend, draw in the family dynamics, including any alcoholism or addictions, conflicts, cut-offs, divorces, etc.

Endnotes

[i] Edwin Chase, "Coping with radical evil in the community of faith," in *Beside Still Waters*. Ed. Stephen Muse (Macon, GA: Smyth and Helwys, 2000), 130.

[ii] John LaRue, "Forced Exits: High Risk Churches," Your Church 42/3 (May/June 1999):72. Cited in Chase, Ibid., 130.

[iii] Ibid., 131

[iv] Norris Smith, "A Survey of Southern Baptist Churches," Sunday School Board of the Southern Baptist Convention (Nashville, TN:1990). Cited in Chase, ibid., 132.

[v] Dallas Willard, *The Divine Conspiracy: Rediscovering Our Hidden Life in God*. (San Francisco: Harpers, 1998), 156-157.

[vi] Michael Emerson and Christian Smith. *Divided by Faith: Evangelical Religion and the Problem of Race in America*. (New York: Oxford University Press, 2000).

*Chapter 11 — I dedicate this chapter to my friends: John, Garry, Richard, Tim, Steve, Ron, Larry and all the others who have been ministry casualties and victims of churches that have abused them. You are truly good men, all of you.

Resources

The following are some helpful books on genograms and how to make them:

Sylvia Shellenberger. Genograms: Assessment and Intervention. W.W. Norton & Company; 2nd edition, 1999.

Genograms: The New Tool for Exploring the Personality, Career, and Love Patterns You Inherit. McGraw-Hill/Contemporary Books, 1989.

Randy Gerson. Genograms in Family Assessment. W.W. Norton & Company; 1st edition, 1986.

I choose to use "board" or "boards" to designate local church lay leadership. Substitute "elders" "trustees" "consistory" or whatever is appropriate for your church.

The following are some books for further reading on the subject of spiritual abuse:

Jeff Vanvonderen. The Subtle Power of Spiritual Abuse. Bethany House, 1992.

Mary Alice Chrnalogar, Twisted Scriptures. Zondervan; Rev. ed., 2000.

Jack Felton. Toxic Faith. Harold Shaw, 2001.

Ken Blue. Healing Spiritual Abuse: How to Break Free from Bad Church Experiences. Intervarsity Press, 1993.

Edwin Chase. "Coping with radical evil in the community of faith," in Beside Still Waters. Ed. Stephen Muse (Macon, GA: Smyth and Helwys, 2000) 130.

John LaRue, "Forced exits: High risk churches," Your Church 42/3 (May/June 1999):72. Cited in Chase, ibid. 130

Ibid., 131

Norris Smith. "A Survey of Southern Baptist Churches," Sunday School Board of the Southern Baptists Convention (Nashville TN:1990) cited in Chase, ibid. 132.

Dallas Willard. The Diviine Conspiracy: Rediscovering Our Hidden Life in God. (San Francisco: Harpers, 1998) 156-157.

Ibid., 157

Michael Emerson and Christian Smith. Divided by Faith: Evangelical Religion and the Problem of Race in America. New York: Oxford University Press, 2000.